Neat Jewish Stuff for Christians

Dr. David Teitelbaum

xulon
PRESS

TABLE OF CONTENTS

Chapter 1: Neat Jewish Stuff for Christians to Consider 7

Chapter 2: Jesus as Prophesied in the Hebrew Scriptures 10

Chapter 3: The Use of Jewish Holy Days in the Mission
of Jesus 23

Chapter 4: Jesus and the Sabbath 30

Chapter 5: Communion, Passover, and the Feast
of Unleavened Bread.. 36

Chapter 6: Using Plagues and Miracles to Overthrow
Pagan Gods 58

Chapter 7: Elijah and John the Baptist 63

Chapter 8: Jesus is Our First Fruits 67

Chapter 9: Why the Holy Spirit Was Sent at Pentecost 75

Chapter 10: Trumpets: The Return of Christ and the
Gathering of Believers 82

Chapter 11: Atonement by Blood... 89

Chapter 12: Dwelling with God: The Feast of Tabernacles 94

Chapter 13: Jesus in the Ancient Tabernacle 99

Chapter 14: Christ and His Bride: Ancient Jewish
    Wedding Customs 117

Appendix 1: Judaism 101: An Overview of Jewish History.... 135
Appendix 2: Questions that Christians Commonly Ask
    About Jews 145
Appendix 3: An Overview of Christian Anti-Semitism 157

Works Consulted 169

CHAPTER 1

Neat Jewish Stuff for Christians to Consider

Knowledge of the Bible and Judaism prior to the birth of Christ is not necessary for salvation or understanding the Christian mission. Yet, consider the following:

1. God could have chosen any people of history to have His Son. He chose the Jews.
2. God could have chosen any woman of earth to bear His Son. He chose a Jew.
3. Jesus was raised Jewish, and much of the symbolism in His parables and teachings comes out of the Jewish culture of His time.
4. His earthly parents were Jewish. John the Baptist was Jewish. All of His disciples were Jewish. Paul was Jewish. The entire early church was Jewish. The donkey He rode

to Jerusalem was Jewish. (Not really ... donkeys aren't Kosher!)

5. The Bible contains sixty-six books. Sixty-four of those books were written by Jews. (Luke, author of the books of Luke and Acts, was a Gentile.)

6. Jesus used Jewish holy days and feasts set down in Leviticus to emphasize many of the essential teachings and salient points of His ministry:

- On the Sabbath, He announced that He was the fulfillment of a prophecy of Isaiah concerning the Messiah.

- On the Feast of Tabernacles, He announced that He was the source of the Holy Spirit, the Living Water.

- On the Feast of Passover, He announced that He was the new Passover Lamb, He gave us communion, and He was crucified.

- On the Feast of Unleavened Bread, He was in the tomb.

- On the Feast of First Fruits, He was resurrected.

- On the Feast of Weeks (Pentecost), He sent the Holy Spirit.

7. Jesus said, "Salvation is from the Jews" (John 4:22).

These are not mere coincidences. Christians grow in worshipful appreciation of Jesus when His roots in Judaism are understood.

CHAPTER 2

Jesus as Prophesied in the Hebrew Scriptures

The Jewish concept of a Messiah involves an anointed one of God coming to usher in an era where humans live together harmoniously and righteously. Interestingly, there is no mention of this Messiah in the five books of Moses. Rabbis believe, however, that the idea is implied in the story of creation. According to Jewish thought, God wanted us to live with Him in a paradise, so He created the Garden of Eden. Human sin required us to be expelled. God did not destroy Eden, however, and is awaiting a time when we will be worthy of return. Judaism asserts that the Messianic Age is the time when we will be brought back to the kind of world that God originally intended. This time is described by many prophets of the Bible, and references to the Messiah can also be found in the Psalms.

Jews believe that the specifics of how God will bring this about are unknown, but in that age there will be no war, no hunger, no greed, no envy and no cruelty. The only occupation of the people of the world will be knowing the Lord. Until that time, Jews believe their mission is to make themselves worthy of the coming of the Messiah.

This is the great point that distinguishes Judaism from Christianity. Christians believe Jesus was the Messiah and that He will return in the future. All other differences between these two great religions grow out of the question of whether or not Jesus was the Anointed One of God, and whether or not His stated path to salvation is truly from God.

That Jesus is clearly and specifically prophesied in the Hebrew Scriptures is an area of significant controversy (presented in greater detail in Appendix 2). The controversy stems primarily from the differing viewpoints that Judaism and Christianity bring to the reading of the Hebrew Bible.

From the Jewish viewpoint, the Bible is approached believing that Jesus is not the Messiah. Jews enter the study of Scripture looking forward, and so they see prophecies of one who is yet to come. Supporting this view, it must be admitted that in reading the Hebrew Bible from beginning to end, one would not conclude that the Messiah would minister for only three years, that no peace or greatness for Israel would come during His ministry, and that the Messiah would then be crucified. Rather, it reads that the Messiah would usher in an era of greatness and peace for the Jews, with Israel being foremost among all the nations.

From the Christian viewpoint, the Bible is approached believing Jesus is the Messiah. Christians enter the study of the Hebrew Bible already having a familiarity with the life and death of Jesus. Looking backwards in Scripture, they see numerous prophecies that validate Jesus as the Messiah who came and will eventually return.

There are over one hundred Hebrew Bible prophecies which are claimed as pointing to Jesus as the Messiah. An exhaustive study of all of these is worth undertaking, but well beyond the scope of this book. We will, however, look at many of the passages and how they relate to the life, mission and ministry of Jesus.

The announcing and preparation for the coming of the Messiah:

From Hebrew Scripture came the tradition that Elijah, a prophet who never died but was taken up to heaven, would return to earth to prepare for the coming of the Messiah. These prophecies find fulfillment in John the Baptist (Matthew 3:3; Mark 1:2-3; Luke 1:17) who came before Jesus. Jesus Himself declares that John the Baptist was indeed the anticipated Elijah (Matthew 11:14, 17:11-13; Mark 9:12).

Malachi 3:1: "See, I will send my messenger, who will prepare the way before me. Then suddenly the Lord you are seeking will come to his temple."

Malachi 4:5: "See, I will send you the prophet Elijah before that great and dreadful day of the Lord comes."

Isaiah 40:3: "A voice of one calling: In the desert prepare the way for the Lord."

The virgin birth:

In the book of Isaiah we find a reference to a young pregnant woman as a sign from God. The disciple Matthew is guided by the Holy Spirit to quote this passage as a foreshadowing of Mary in his Gospel (Matthew 1:23). The name Immanuel means "God with us," and points to Jesus.

Isaiah 7:14: "Therefore the Lord himself will give you a sign: The virgin will be with child and will give birth to a son, and you will call him Immanuel."

Birth location:

Jesus was born in the town of Bethlehem, which is located in the region of Ephrathah (Matthew 2:6).

Micah 5:2: "But you, Bethlehem Ephrathah, though you are small among the clans of Judah, out of you will come for me one who will be ruler over Israel, whose origins are from old, from ancient times."

Messianic lineage:

The Messiah was foretold to be from the line of Jacob, from the tribe of Judah, and a descendant of King David, whose father was Jesse. The following prophecies find fulfillment in the lineage of Jesus' earthly father, Joseph (Matthew 1:1-16), and in the lineage of His mother, Mary (Luke 3:23-37).

Numbers 24:17: "A star will come out of Jacob..."

Micah 5:2: "Though you are small among the clans of Judah, out of you will come one for me who will be ruler over Israel."

2 Samuel 7:12-13 [Spoken in prophecy to David]*: "When your days are over and you rest with your fathers, I will raise up your offspring to succeed you, who will come from your own body, and I will establish his kingdom. He is the one who will build a house for my Name, and I will establish the throne of his kingdom forever."*

Isaiah 11:1-2: "A shoot will come up from the stump of Jesse; from his roots a Branch will bear fruit. The Spirit of the Lord will rest on him."

Messianic titles:

Many of the titles used for Jesus are found in messianic prophecy. "Mighty God" and "Everlasting Father" would apply only to one who had divine power.

Isaiah 9:6: "For unto us a child is born, to us a son is given, and the government will be on his shoulders. And he will be called Wonderful Counselor, Mighty God, Everlasting Father, Prince of Peace. Of the increase of his government and peace there will be no end. He will reign on David's throne and over his kingdom, establishing and upholding it with justice and righteousness from that time on and forever."

Return from Egypt:

When the Jews first went to Egypt, they were very few in number. After multiplying greatly, they were enslaved for 400 years and then God delivered them.

Hosea 11:1: "When Israel was a child, I loved him, and out of Egypt I called my son."

While Hosea is referring here to God calling the Israelites out of Egypt, we find Matthew seeing the history of Israel reflected in the life of Jesus (Matthew 2:15). Thus, as Israel entered Egypt as an infant nation and was later brought out under the direction of God, so Jesus was taken to Egypt as an infant and was also later brought out under the direction of God.

Healings:

Matthew refers to this prophecy in Matthew 8:17, after he reports some of the healings performed by Jesus.

Isaiah 53:4: "Surely he took up our infirmities and carried our sorrows."

In Matthew 11: 5 Jesus tells the followers of John the Baptist to go back and report on the healings of the blind and the deaf that they have seen.

Isaiah 29:18: In that day the deaf will hear the words of the scroll, and out of gloom and darkness the eyes of the blind will see. Once more the humble will rejoice in the Lord; the needy will rejoice in the Holy One of Israel."

On being a servant of God to the nations:

Out of a chapter replete with messianic prophecy, we find this quoted in Matthew 12:18.

Isaiah 42:1: "Here is my servant, whom I uphold, my chosen one in whom I delight; I will put my Spirit on him and he will bring justice to the nations."

On going to the Gentiles:

Matthew quotes Isaiah as he describes the preaching of Jesus in Galilee (Matthew 4:15-16).

Isaiah: 42:6: "I, the Lord, have called you in righteous-
ness; I will take hold of your hand. I will keep you and
will make you to be a covenant for the people and a light
before the Gentiles."

Isaiah 9:1-2: "But in the future he will honor Galilee of
the Gentiles, by the way of the sea, along the Jordan - The
people walking in darkness have seen a great light; on
those living in the land of the shadow of death a light has
dawned."

On introducing a New Covenant:

At the last supper, Jesus introduced a New Covenant (Luke
22: 20).

Jeremiah 31: 31-34: "The time is coming when I will
make a new covenant with the house of Israel and with
the house of Judah. It will not be like the covenant I made
with their forefathers when I took them by the hand to
lead them out of Egypt."

Jesus is rejected:

Jesus quotes a Psalm about Himself, referring to His rejection
by the Jewish religious leaders (Matthew 21:42).

Psalm 118:22: "The stone the builders rejected has
become the capstone; the Lord has done this, and it is
marvelous in our eyes."

Jesus claims to be David's Lord:

Jesus used a quote from Psalms to explain to the Pharisees that David, speaking by the Spirit, recognized Him as Lord (Mark 12:36). Jesus was claiming that as the Messiah, He was much more than just a descendant of David; He was actually David's Lord.

Psalm 110:1: "The Lord says to my Lord: 'Sit at my right hand until I make your enemies a footstool for your feet.'"

The entry into Jerusalem:

With great rejoicing of the people, Jesus has a triumphal ride into Jerusalem on a donkey (Matthew 21:5).

Zechariah 9:9: "Rejoice greatly, O Daughter of Zion! Shout, Daughter of Jerusalem! See, your king comes to you, righteous and having salvation, gentle and riding on a donkey, on a colt, the foal of a donkey."

Jesus is betrayed for 30 pieces of silver:

Judas agreed to help in the arrest of Jesus for the payment of 30 pieces of silver (Matthew 26:15). He later regretted his action, threw his coins into the Temple and then hanged himself. The chief priests used the money to buy a potter's field as a burial place (Matthew 27: 3-7).

Zechariah 11:12-13: "So they paid me thirty pieces of silver. And the Lord said to me, 'Throw it to the potter' - the handsome price at which they priced me! So I took the thirty pieces of silver and threw them into the house of the Lord to the potter."

Jesus is deserted by His followers:

Both chapters 12 and 13 of Zechariah are about the final days of the Messiah and are relevant here. This particular passage is referenced by Jesus as He warns the disciples about His imminent arrest (Matthew 26:31).

Zechariah 13:7: "Strike the shepherd, and the sheep will be scattered."

The trial of Jesus:

Jesus offered no defense during His trial before Pilate. After the trial, He was flogged. Then the soldiers mocked Him, spat on Him, and hit Him on the head (Matthew 27:12-14, 26-31).

Isaiah 53:7: "He was oppressed and afflicted, yet he did not open his mouth; he was led like a lamb to the slaughter."

Isaiah 50:6: "I offered my back to those who beat me, my cheeks to those who pulled out my beard; I did not hide my face from mocking and spitting."

Jesus and the crucifixion:

A number of writings in the Prophets and Psalms refer with astonishing accuracy to the events of the Crucifixion. These take on even greater significance when we recognize that punishment by crucifixion originated well after these prophecies were written. A number of crucifixion prophecies are found in Psalm 22, which begins with Jesus' final words on the cross, "My God, My God, why have you forsaken me?" (Matthew 27:46). Since the Jews of the time of Jesus regularly used the book of Psalms as a prayer book, the calling out of the opening lines of Psalm 22 by Jesus can be seen as His way of prompting those present to review it.

We read a strikingly accurate account of the taunts hurled at Jesus at the crucifixion (Matthew 27:42).

Psalm 22:7: "All who see me mock me; they hurl insults, shaking their heads. He trusts in the Lord; let the Lord rescue him. Let him deliver him, since he delights in him."

When the side of Jesus is pierced by a Roman spear, water comes out (John 19:34). His bones would be dislodged from hanging on the cross.

Psalm 22:14: "I am poured out like water, all my bones are out of joint."

Psalm 22:16: "They have pierced my hands and feet."

Roman soldiers in charge of crucifixion were entitled to the clothing of the prisoners. It is recorded that the Romans cast lots for Jesus' garments (Matthew 27:35).

Psalm 22:18: "They divide my garments among them and cast lots for my clothing."

An attempt was made to give Jesus vinegar to drink during His time on the cross. (Matthew 27:34, 48).

Psalm 69:21: "They put gall in my food and gave me vinegar for my thirst."

Jesus and His burial:

Jesus was crucified as a criminal along with other criminals ("the wicked"), and then buried in the tomb of a wealthy man (Matthew 27:57-60).

Isaiah 53:9: "He was assigned a grave with the wicked, and with the rich in his death."

The return of the Messiah:

Jesus said, "But I say to all of you: In the future you will see the Son of Man sitting at the right hand of the Mighty One and coming on the clouds of heaven" (Matthew 26:64).

Daniel 7:13: "In my vision at night I looked, and there before me was one like a son of man, coming with the clouds of heaven. He approached the Ancient of Days and was led into his presence."

A summary of the life and mission of Jesus:

This is found in the Hebrew Scriptures in the book of Isaiah, chapter 53. The reader is encouraged to look at this chapter for further insights.

CHAPTER 2 QUESTIONS FOR DISCUSSION

1. Which of the prophecies presented was most significant to you? Why?

2. Read Psalm 22. What are some reasons that Jesus, while on the cross, might cry out, "My God, My God, why have you forsaken me?"

3. Read Matthew 26:15, Matthew 27:3-7, and Zechariah 11:12-13. Keeping in mind that Zechariah spoke his prophecy 500 years before the birth of Jesus, what do you find most meaningful about it?

4. Read Appendix 2, section 3. How would you answer the question, "Since Israel did not become a great nation during the life of Jesus, how could He be the promised Messiah?" How would you respond to the challenge that Isaiah 7:14 does not specifically designate a virgin birth?

CHAPTER 3

The Use of Jewish Holy Days in the Mission of Jesus

Once God had delivered the Jews from slavery in Egypt, about 1500 B.C., He set about sculpting them into a people unique in the world. In a world of polytheistic cultures, they were to remain distinctly monotheistic. Surrounded by cultures of immorality and hedonism, they were to abide by a strict legal code that directed behavior, morality and ethics. Alone in a pagan world, they were to follow a unique system of worship as dictated by their one true God through Moses.

The structure for this worship was based on a series of holy festivals, each of which had a special meaning and a unique set of rituals. We find meticulous instructions for celebrating each of these in the Hebrew Scriptures. In Leviticus 23, the feasts are concisely listed:

• The Sabbath

- The Passover
- The Feast of Unleavened Bread
- First Fruits
- The Feast of Weeks, also known as Pentecost
- The Feast of Trumpets
- The Day of Atonement
- The Feast of Tabernacles

Besides the Sabbath, which occurs weekly, the holy days are divided into four feasts that take place in the spring and three that occur in the fall. In the mission of Jesus, the four spring feasts symbolize events that took place when He was on earth:

- He gave us Communion and was crucified at Passover.
- He was placed in the tomb on the Feast of Unleavened Bread.
- He was resurrected at First Fruits.
- He sent the Holy Spirit to us at the Feast of Weeks (Pentecost).

The three fall feasts symbolize events that are to be fulfilled on His return:

- The Feast of Trumpets represents the return of Christ and the gathering of believers.
- The Day of Atonement will mark the final Day of Judgment.

- The Feast of Tabernacles marks the return of Christ to dwell with us again.

On the feasts of Unleavened Bread, Feast of Weeks, and Tabernacles, God commanded all of the Jews to present themselves before Him. In the time of Jesus, this required all Jews to make a pilgrimage to Jerusalem for each of these three events. Thus, 1,500 years in advance, God set up large audiences in Jerusalem for several of the major events of the ministry of Jesus. The city would have been filled on the Feast of Tabernacles, when He announced that He is the source of living water: the Holy Spirit. It would have been filled for Unleavened Bread for the Crucifixion and Resurrection. It would have been filled for the coming of the Holy Spirit at the Feast of Weeks (Pentecost).

With humility and awe, we can see the symbolism of these observances richly incorporated into the ministry of Jesus. With admiring wonder, we realize that the plan for the life of Christ was set in motion 1,500 years in advance.

We will consider each of the holy days in some detail, but certain points should be understood beforehand. The times of celebrating each of these feasts were based on the Jewish calendar, an agricultural calendar based on the 28-day cycle of the moon. The Western world utilizes the solar calendar year, based on the 365 days it takes for the earth to revolve around the sun. However, the Jews still date their holy days by the original lunar calendar as commanded by God. This explains why the Jewish holidays seem to vary as to the month in which they are celebrated each year.

Furthermore, Jewish holy days begin at sunset. The Sabbath, for example, begins at sundown on Friday evening and continues until sundown Saturday. This custom comes from the Creation account in Genesis 1. The first day of Creation ends with the statement, "And there was evening and there was morning - the first day." All the following days end in the same wording. Recognizing that God denotes His days from evening until morning, Jews celebrate their holy days the same way.

A number of the holy day observances are associated with specific sacrifices, and as we study these we will see that the sacrifices also have great significance in the life of Jesus. From the beginning of Judaism, God required sacrifices to make atonement. Try as he might, man's inherent tendency to sin would always cause his behavior to fall short of God's commanded ideal. Thus, God provided a system to allow man to become righteous before God: a system in which sacrifices would be offered as acts of atonement from both intentional and unintentional sin. Furthermore, as awful as it seems in our modern society, atonement could only be achieved through the shedding of blood. Sacrifices offered for other causes, such as for worship and thanksgiving, could be made from grains or fruit.

Christians often wonder what happened to these sacrifices, and how the Jews seek atonement today. Remembering Jewish history, the Temple was destroyed by the Romans during the First Jewish Revolt in 70 A.D. This was the only site in which the sacrifices could be performed. This situation was not without precedent, however. After the Temple of Solomon was destroyed in 586 B.C., the Jews were forced into exile in Babylonia. The exiled prophet Daniel prayed fervently during the exile (Daniel 6:10). Following this model, the rabbis in the first century after the destruction of the Temple substituted prayer for blood sacrifices complemented by study of God's Word, ethical behavior and charitable acts. The synagogue would take the place of the Temple as the central place of worship, and the rabbis would serve as the religious leaders. Judaism thus changed from the God-ordained sacrificial system into Rabbinical Judaism over the following 150 years. From that time until the present day, prayer, the study of God's word, ethical behavior and charitable acts take the place of sacrifices in making atonement with God.

Yet even though the Jews no longer make sacrifices today, they were doing so in the time of Jesus. We will study the sacrifices to help us fully comprehend the essential mission of Jesus, as God applied the symbolism in His life.

As we review the Hebrew Scriptures, we see that specific sacrifices were commanded for different occasions and different reasons. The required sacrifices might include live animals, grain or wine. The animals had to be free from blemish or defect. The grain might be in the form of finely milled flour or baked into a cake. This cake might be required to have yeast or oil, or specifically stated to be free of yeast or oil.

To apply this knowledge to the life and ministry of Jesus, we should recognize the following symbolism:

- Animals without defect represent a sinless state.
- Blood shed in the sacrifices was considered sacred. We are told in the Bible that the life of a creature is in the blood, and God gives it to us to make atonement for our life (Leviticus 17:11). This atonement by blood was understood to be the substitution of one life for another.
- Yeast in the Bible represents sin. Bread without yeast is called unleavened bread, and represents a sinless state.
- Oil in the Bible represents anointing with the Holy Spirit of God.
- Wine represents joy, gratitude or devotion.

As we will see, the feasts themselves, as well as their specific sacrifices, hold rich meaning for the Christian who sees in them the mission of Christ.

CHAPTER 3 QUESTIONS FOR DISCUSSION

1. God wanted the Jews to live very different lives from the people around them. These differences included behaviors

and beliefs. How would the same ideas apply to modern Christians?

2. Why do you think God orchestrated the key events of the life and ministry of Jesus to occur at the times of the ancient Jewish festivals? What does this mean to you as an individual?

3. The four spring feasts found symbolic fulfillment during the life of Jesus. The three fall feasts will be fulfilled when He returns. What do you think the summer and winter seasons, both without holy days, symbolize?

4. Why would God ordain that animal sacrifices must be without blemish, and grain offerings must be made without yeast?

5. Read Leviticus 17:11. How does this passage lay a foundation for Christianity?

CHAPTER 4

Jesus and the Sabbath

We begin looking at the feasts of Israel with the Sabbath, which is unique in many ways. While all of the other feasts are celebrated annually, the Sabbath is celebrated weekly. It is a holy day in which God Himself participated, for we read in Genesis 2:3 that "God blessed the seventh day and made it holy, because on it He rested from all the work of creating that He had done."

The Sabbath is first mentioned as a holy day observance in Exodus, just after the Jews are delivered from slavery in Egypt. The Hebrews were required to daily go out and collect the manna God provided for them to eat because it would spoil overnight. However, on the sixth day of each week, they could gather a double portion of manna, which did not spoil for two days. This allowed them to do no work on the seventh day of each week. For a people who had been enslaved 400 years, suddenly having a day off every week must have been quite a treat!

The Sabbath is the only feast mentioned in the Ten Commandments: "Observe the Sabbath day by keeping it holy, as the Lord your God has commanded you" (Deuteronomy 5:12). In a zealous attempt to strictly keep this commandment, a number of restrictions were developed by Jewish interpreters of the law, and by the time of Jesus these were quite cumbersome. For example, it was determined just how far one could walk on the Sabbath. No work was to be done, including the lighting of fires or the carrying of objects. No medical care was to be provided unless it was feared that the afflicted person would die before the next day.

Jesus regularly celebrated the Sabbath. He would often go to the synagogue on the Sabbath to teach, "as was his custom" (Luke 4:16). On one such occasion, early in His ministry, Jesus observed the Sabbath by attending the synagogue in Nazareth, the town in which He was raised (Luke 4:16-30). He was given the honor of reading from the Hebrew Scriptures. Opening the scroll to Isaiah 61:1-2, He read the following messianic prophecy:

"The Spirit of the Lord is on me, because he has anointed me to preach good news to the poor. He has sent me to proclaim freedom for the prisoners and recovery of sight for the blind, to release the oppressed, to proclaim the year of the Lord's favor."

The "year of the Lord's favor" would refer to the time when salvation would be proclaimed in the Messianic Age.

Jesus then astonished the crowd by saying, "Today this scripture is fulfilled in your hearing." He was declaring that He was the fulfillment of this messianic prophecy.

The reaction was initially favorable, yet they challenged His authority by questioning how one of their own neighbors could be the Messiah. Jesus then angered them by stating that no prophet is accepted in his hometown. He related two scriptural instances (Elijah and Elisha) in which prophets sent by God gave aid to Gentiles but not to Jews. This infuriated the people so much that they drove Him out of town and tried to throw Him off a cliff. Jesus, however, walked "right through the crowd and went on his way."

On that special Sabbath in Nazareth, Jesus declared Himself to be the Messiah. He also reminded the Israelites that should they continue to reject Him, God would send Him to the Gentiles, as in the cases of Elijah and Elisha.

During other times in His ministry, He challenged the strict dictates and teachings of the Jewish religious leadership regarding Sabbath observance, and even challenged their very authority. His challenges to the customs of the day can be summarized by reviewing three defining statements that He made:

- "It is lawful to do good on the Sabbath" (Matthew 12:12).

- "The Sabbath was made for man, not man for the Sabbath" (Mark 2:27).
- "The Son of Man is Lord even of the Sabbath" (Mark 2:28).

These statements, the third of which would have been considered blasphemous, challenged the authority of the Jewish religious leadership. Sabbath observances became a major point of contention between Jesus and the religious authorities.

Jesus held the position that work of a godly nature was permissible under God's law. For example, Jesus performed several miraculous healings on the Sabbath. The Pharisees challenged Him on this, holding to their position that healing was a form of work and thus prohibited unless the person was in danger of dying without care. None of the healings of Jesus undertaken on the Sabbath were of a critical nature, so the Pharisees held that He should postpone such healings until the Sabbath had passed.

In Matthew 12:9-12, we read that the Pharisees actually set Jesus up for such a controversy when they asked Him in the synagogue if it was lawful to heal on the Sabbath. There was a man present who had a shriveled hand. Jesus pointed out that the leaders themselves would lift one of their own sheep out of a pit should the animal fall in on a Sabbath. Reminding them that a man is more valuable than a sheep, He concluded with, "Therefore it is lawful to do good on the Sabbath." He then healed the man so that the shriveled hand was completely restored.

In Mark 2:23-28, Jesus was challenged because on the Sabbath His disciples were spotted picking heads of grain to eat. Technically speaking, the disciples were harvesting, which was against Sabbath law. Here Jesus reminded the Pharisees that their revered ancestor, King David, when fleeing the wrath of Saul, ate bread that was consecrated and therefore unlawful for him to eat (1 Samuel 21:1-6). In both instances, godly men were doing something physically necessary for life. Therefore, doing that which is physically necessary for life is not against the laws of God, even if done on the Sabbath. Jesus drives this point home by saying, "The Sabbath was made for man, not man for the Sabbath." He then added a statement they would have considered blasphemous, "So the Son of Man is Lord even of the Sabbath."

In saying this, Jesus was publicly claiming not only to be a higher authority than the Pharisees, but to be Lord over a holy day given specifically to the Jews by God.

CHAPTER 4 QUESTIONS FOR DISCUSSION

1. Orthodox Jews maintain a strict observance of the Sabbath to this day, staying at home with their families from sunset Friday until sunset Saturday, except for joining in prayer

at the synagogue on Saturday. How would it impact Christianity if we did the same?

2. Jesus regularly observed the Sabbath, and made the following three statements:
   - "It is lawful to do good on the Sabbath."
   - "The Sabbath was made for man, not man for the Sabbath."
   - "The Son of Man is Lord even of the Sabbath."

How do these statements affect your life and your feelings about the Sabbath?

3. What in the prophecy of Isaiah 61:1-2 is significant to you?

4. Has there been a time in your life when you felt like a rejected prophet in your own hometown?

CHAPTER 5

Communion, Passover and the Feast of Unleavened Bread

Of all the feasts, Passover is the richest with meaning for Christians. Jesus knew that the Passover would be His last earthly meal. He knew that in less than 24 hours, He would be crucified. It was at this dinner that He gave us Communion. In this He was offering His wedding proposal to His bride — the disciples, who represented the church. As leader of the ceremonial meal, He would have explained the symbolism of the Passover foods and told the story of God's deliverance from slavery in Egypt. He used this opportunity to explain that He was the new Passover lamb, and that His death would bring deliverance from slavery to sin.

Passover was celebrated by the Jews for 1,500 years before Jesus. The feast commemorates their deliverance from slavery in Egypt. The feast of Unleavened Bread started the day after Passover and continued for seven additional days. Although the two are distinct events as directed in Leviticus, they are basically celebrated as one holiday, and we will study them as such.

To fully understand the message of Jesus at that last supper 2,000 years ago, we must comprehend the full story of God's deliverance of the Jews from slavery in Egypt, and also recognize the Christian symbolism in the Passover foods and customs.

History of the Holiday

One might wonder how the Jews came to be slaves in Egypt; a review of Biblical history is useful here. Abraham fathered Isaac, and Isaac fathered Jacob. Jacob had sons who ultimately fathered the twelve tribes of Israel. One of Jacob's sons, Joseph, was gifted in dream interpretation. In a classic example of poor parenting, Jacob showed obvious favoritism toward Joseph. He gave him an elaborate cloak, which symbolized his authority over his brothers, even though he was one of the youngest. His brothers grew jealous of Joseph and sold him as a slave to a caravan headed for Egypt. Joseph had many adventures and misadventures in Egypt, but ultimately he had the opportunity to interpret a troubling dream of the Pharaoh. This interpretation saved Egypt from a seven-year famine. In gratitude, Pharaoh granted Joseph great honor and power. Joseph invited his father and brothers to Egypt, thereby saving them from the famine. He forgave his brothers and they lived there in peace and prosperity for many years. Since the Jews were comfortable and prospering, they did not leave

Egypt. Remaining there was in violation of God's covenant with Abraham, however, since He had given them the land of Israel as the place where they were to live.

After a time, a new Pharaoh arose "who did not know about Joseph" (Exodus 1:8). Concerned over the rapidly growing number of Jews, and fearing that they might join the enemies of Egypt, he made them slaves. The lives of the Hebrews were made bitter with hard labor in building cities and working in the fields. Still, they continued to reproduce in large numbers.

Now fearing that the growing slave population might join an enemy force, Pharaoh decreed that all newborn male children would be put to death. Into this situation, Moses was born. To avoid having her son murdered, Moses' mother put him in a basket and floated him down the Nile River. He was found by Pharaoh's daughter and adopted. He was thus raised as an Egyptian prince and was taught many skills that he would need for the future.

But Moses grew up feeling a kinship for the Hebrews. He saw their suffering and had compassion for them. One day he intervened in an injustice and killed an Egyptian taskmaster. Even a prince did not have the right to do this, so he ran away into the desert. While in the desert, he encountered some shepherds and married a daughter of the group and began living as one of them.

While tending sheep one day, he saw a bush that was burning but not consumed. When he investigated, God spoke to him from within the bush and gave him instructions for liberating his people from Egyptian slavery.

Returning to Egypt, Moses had an audience with Pharaoh, who laughed at the request to let the Jews go. To change Pharaoh's heart, God sent a series of ten plagues. With each plague, Pharaoh had the opportunity to avoid further carnage by letting the Jews go free, yet his heart remained hard. The first nine plagues brought Egypt to material ruin. The tenth was to cause the most suffering: Death of all the firstborn in Egypt. The Jews were warned by God (through Moses) about this last plague and how they could avoid the death of their own firstborn. They were told to take a lamb without blemish into their homes and keep it for four days. Then they were to slaughter it and sprinkle the doorposts and lintel of the doorways of their houses with the blood, using a hyssop branch as a brush. Finally they were to cook the lamb and eat it, while standing fully dressed and prepared to depart the country. As God passed over Egypt, smiting all the firstborn of the Egyptians, the Hebrews were protected by the blood of the lamb on their doorways.

After this horrible plague, which claimed the life of Pharaoh's own son, he relented and agreed to let the Hebrews go. God moved the hearts of the Egyptians to be favorable to the Jews so that they gave them much gold, silver, and fine linen. These materials were essential to the later construction of the Tabernacle.

As the Hebrews left Egypt, they did not have time to prepare food, so they made bread quickly without allowing it to rise. This ushered in the custom of eating unleavened bread at this holiday, called the "bread of affliction" in remembrance of their enslavement.

Passover Today

For 3,500 years, Passover has been celebrated by Jews throughout the world with very little change to the commanded ceremonies and customs over the centuries. On the first night there is a ceremonial feast called a *Seder*. The next seven days after Passover constitute the holiday of Unleavened Bread. On these days, no products made with yeast are to be consumed. Only unleavened bread, called *matzah*, may be eaten during Passover and the Feast of Unleavened Bread.

Preparations for Passover begin well before the actual holiday. It is essential that the house be cleansed of all leaven, or *hametz*, including crumbs. To serve this purpose, a ritual has developed in which the father and his children seek out the crumbs, gather them, and the crumbs are burned in the fireplace. The entire house is thoroughly cleaned and the dishes must also be ceremonially cleansed for the event.

At the Seder dinner, the story of God's deliverance from slavery in Egypt is told. The dinner is guided by a book entitled *The Haggadah*, which means "The Telling." It is emphasized that each Jew is to consider that he himself was liberated from slavery in Egypt directly by God, and that this story is also his individual story.

Special symbolic foods are eaten to remind the Jews of the various parts of the deliverance. At the dinner, these foods are arranged attractively on a Seder plate. Three of these foods are specifically designated in Exodus 12:8: "They are to eat the meat (Passover lamb) roasted over the fire, along with bitter herbs, and bread made without yeast." The other ceremonial foods have been added over the years by custom. In addition to the special foods, there are a number of traditions that have special meanings of interest.

We will now walk through a Seder ceremony, reviewing those foods and customs that Jesus used symbolically to teach His disciples during His last meal with them.

The Seder Ceremony

The evening begins as the head of the household takes his place at the head of the table. Near him will be a Seder plate containing a small amount of each of the ceremonial foods. This man will be functioning as the high priest over the rituals that will take place on this holy night in his home. He will be the one to direct the service. He will lift up the ceremonial foods from the Passover plate and offer blessings over them as each is explained in the service. In his capacity as high priest, he might wear a white ceremonial robe called a *kittle*.

It is common to begin the evening with a few welcoming words to the guests. At His last supper, Jesus said, "I have eagerly desired to eat this Passover with you before I suffer" (Luke 22:15).

Ceremonies begin as candles are lit and blessed by the mother of the house.

Four cups of wine will be consumed this evening. While wine always symbolizes joy, each of these cups has an additional special significance and a special name. Officially starting the service, the first is the Cup of Sanctification. Acting as high priest, the head of the household confirms that all Passover preparations are satisfactory as he drinks this cup.

Following the Cup of Sanctification is the ceremony of the washing of the hands. In Exodus 19:6, the Israelites are instructed to be a "kingdom of priests and a holy nation." In Temple times, the priests had a number of hand-washing rituals. It is in filling this role that all present undergo a ceremonial washing of the hands as a bowl of water is passed around the table. It was at this point that Jesus "took off his outer clothing, and wrapped a towel around his waist. After that, He poured water into a basin and began to wash his disciples' feet, drying them with the towel that was wrapped around him" (John 13:4-6).

Washing of feet was never a part of the Seder. It was, however, a custom in Middle Eastern hospitality to have slaves wash the feet of visitors. Here, on a holiday that celebrates deliverance by God from slavery into freedom, we have the Son of God voluntarily dressing as a slave and acting as a slave to His disciples. After all had their feet washed, Jesus said, "Do you understand what I have done for you? You call me 'Teacher' and 'Lord,' and rightly so, for that is what I am. Now that I, your Lord and Teacher, have washed your feet, you also should wash one another's feet. I have set you an example that you should do as I have done for you. I tell you the truth, no servant is greater than his master, nor is a messenger greater than the one who sent him. Now that you know these things, you will be blessed if you do them" (John 13:12-17). By this very humble act, the Son of God was showing us that those who follow him will be blessed if they serve one another with great humility.

After the washing of the hands is the eating of the parsley, or *karpas*. The leaves of the parsley sprig serve as a reminder that lamb's blood was sprinkled on the doorposts of the houses, using a branch of the hyssop plant. The parsley is dipped in salt water before eating, signifying the tears shed by the enslaved Hebrews.

The *matzah tash* and the *afikomen* — now this is an interesting custom indeed! On the Seder table is a linen pouch called a matzah tash. The pouch has three pockets. A piece of matzah is placed in each pocket. At this point in the service, the middle matzah is removed from its pocket and broken in half. One of the halves is called the afikomen. The afikomen is placed in a white linen napkin and hidden. We will see that later in the service there is a search by the children to find it.

The Four Questions are next. A favored tradition is to have the youngest able child read or recite the four questions. They begin with, "How different is this night from all other nights!" Then the questions are asked: "On all other nights we eat bread or matzah. On this night why do we eat only matzah?" "On all other nights we eat all kinds of vegetables. On this night why do we eat only bitter herbs?" "On all other nights we do not dip our vegetables even once. On this night why do we dip them twice?" "On all other nights we eat our meal either sitting or reclining. On this night why do we eat only reclining?" These questions are answered as the Passover story is told and as the ceremonial foods are eaten.

Prolonged readings now begin. Not only is the story of God's redemption from slavery related, but many rabbinical commentaries from centuries past are added. Some paragraphs are read in unison, and most families alternate readers by going around the table. In this way, all have a chance to participate.

During the readings it is stated several times that once we were slaves, and now we are free. This explains the question of why we eat reclining, for slaves had to stand at attention during meals. Only free men had the luxury of reclining. To emphasize the point, many Jewish families bring pillows to the table to lean on in joyful appreciation of freedom.

The Cup of Plagues is now used to remember how God redeemed His people out of slavery by visiting ten plagues upon the Egyptians. Interestingly, as each plague is named, a drop is spilled from this cup. Remembering that wine symbolizes joy, in this custom we lessen our joy in God's deliverance by having compassion for those who suffered from the plagues, even though they harmed us. This is in keeping with the Biblical warning of Proverbs 24:17-18: "Do not gloat when your enemy falls; when he stumbles, do not let your heart rejoice, or the Lord will see and disapprove." It is worth noting that the Hebrew word for Egypt occurs more than 700 times in the Bible. Only the name Israel occurs more frequently. Yet none of the references to Egypt are derogatory!

After the ten drops are spilled, the readings continue. There is an extensive explanation of the plagues and the awesomeness of God's deliverance. Then the readings turn to the explanation of the three biblically commanded Passover foods: the Passover offering (the lamb), the unleavened bread, and the bitter herbs.

The Passover lamb is now represented by the shank bone of a lamb found on the Passover plate. It is explained that the sacrifice of a lamb was necessary for the Lord to "pass over" the houses of the children of Israel in Egypt when He smote the firstborn of the Egyptians. From the first Passover until the destruction of the Temple in 70 A.D., a lamb was ceremonially sacrificed for each household in Jerusalem. Since the destruction of the Temple, lamb is no longer eaten at the Passover dinner, but the shank bone is placed on the plate as a reminder. Jesus used the symbolism of the Passover lamb in giving us Communion, as we will see.

The leader of the Seder next holds up a piece of the unleavened bread, or *matzah*. This is the second of the biblically commanded foods. We are told that the Hebrews had to leave Egypt in such haste that there was no time to let the bread rise, and so it is called the Bread of Affliction. This answers the question of why we eat only matzah at this season.

In the Bible, yeast is symbolic of sin. It is most closely related to the sin of pride, for yeast puffs bread up just as pride puffs man up. Unleavened bread, then, symbolizes not having sin. Christians believe the only one to live a sinless life was Jesus. How fitting, then, that He chose unleavened bread to give us the gift of Communion. The Apostle Paul realized this when he wrote, "Your boasting is not good. Don't you know that a little yeast works through the whole batch of dough? Get rid of the old yeast that you may be a new batch without yeast — as you really are. For Christ, our Passover lamb, has been sacrificed. Therefore let us keep the Festival |Unleavened Bread|, not with the old yeast, the yeast of malice and wickedness, but with bread without yeast, the bread of sincerity and truth" (1 Corinthians 5:6-8).

Haroset is eaten next. It is a mixture of apples and nuts, which in physical appearance, resembles the mortar used in building cities for Pharaoh. The sweetness reminds us of the sweetness of

God's redemption. The matzah is dipped in the haroset and eaten. Though not a biblically mandated food, it is everyone's favorite.

The bitter herbs, usually horseradish, are the third of the biblically commanded foods of Passover. It is to remind us of the bitterness of slavery. The bitter herbs are picked up on a piece of matzah and dipped into the haroset, then eaten. This answers the question of why we dip our vegetables twice. We have already dipped the parsley into the salt water, signifying tears of sadness in slavery. Now we dip the bitter herbs, reminding us of the bitterness of bondage. Yet this time it is not dipped in salt water but in the sweet haroset to remind Jews of the sweetness of life in freedom after slavery.

It was at this point in the Seder that Jesus, two millennia ago, identified Judas as the one who would betray Him. "While they were reclining at the table eating, he said, 'I tell you the truth, one of you will betray me-one who is eating with me.' They were saddened and one by one they said to him, 'Surely not I?' 'It is one of the Twelve,' he replied, 'one who dips bread into the bowl with me'" (Mark 14:18-20). It was at this point that Jesus dismissed Judas from the dinner. The treason was a bitter experience for Jesus, for Judas had followed the Lord for three years as a friend and disciple. It was also bitter for Judas, who later recognized his mistake and hung himself. Yet, there is sweetness here, for the treason was necessary for believers to know freedom from sin. As Judas was dismissed from the dinner, he was also dismissed from the congregation of the disciples. Significantly, he missed the first Communion.

There is a small but confusing point for some Christians concerning how the disciples could be reclining while eating, and how John could lean back against Jesus. We read in John 13:22-25, "His disciples stared at one another, at a loss to know which of them he meant. One of them, the disciple whom Jesus loved, was reclining next to him. Simon Peter motioned to this disciple and said, 'Ask him which one he means.' Leaning back against Jesus, he asked him, 'Lord, who is it?'"

We have already discussed the custom of reclining at the meal. In fact, this was a customary way of eating in the Middle East at that time. The table would probably have been L-shaped, and low to the ground by our modern standards. The honored leader of the Seder would have the position at the corner of the L. It was customary to have the youngest of ceremonial age immediately to the right of the leader. (Think of a Jewish grandfather with his 13-year old grandson next to him). Rather than sitting in chairs, the disciples would have been on pillows or mats, in lying position, propped up on their left elbow. The right hand would have been used for eating. (Even to this day, in some Middle Eastern and African cultures where clean water for hand washing is scarce, body hygiene is performed with the left hand while the right is used for eating.) So we have the leader of the Seder, Jesus, reclining at the corner of the table, and the youngest disciple, John, reclining next to Him. It would be a natural movement for John to lean back against Jesus to ask a question.

Following the eating of bitter herbs, a delicious Passover meal is served. Often the food includes favored ethnic dishes, such as matzah ball soup or gefilte fish. All dishes must be completely free of leaven products. This has allowed for the creation of some very creative Jewish delicacies, such as cakes made with matzah instead of flour.

After dinner, the children search for the afikomen. This is the broken piece of matzah that was hidden earlier, wrapped in a white linen napkin. As the Passover ceremony cannot end without it, there is a reward for the child who finds it and brings it back to the table.

Let us take a look at this interesting custom of the matzah and the afikomen. We looked earlier at the pouch with three pockets, called a *matzah tash*, which is on the Passover table. In it are three pieces of matzah. This item was not present at the time of Jesus, and there is only speculation as to why Jews have a matzah tash in every home to this day. The rabbis speculate that the three matzah may represent the three patriarchs, Abraham, Isaac and Jacob. Yet why would the middle one, Isaac, be broken, wrapped in a white linen napkin, hidden, and recovered? The same is true for another rabbinical theory that perhaps the three matzah represent the three groups of the Hebrews: the priests, Levites and the people. Again, why would the Levites be broken, wrapped in a white linen napkin, hidden, and recovered?

It is possible that this custom was introduced into the Passover Seder shortly after the time of Jesus by the early believers. The matzah tash can be seen as an astonishing representation of the Trinity. If the three matzah represent the Father, Son and Holy Spirit, then the middle matzah is the Son. The middle matzah, representing the Son, is first taken out of the pouch. This represents Jesus leaving His place among the Trinity to come to earth in human form. His body is then broken to represent the Crucifixion. The body is then wrapped in white linen cloth to represent Jesus being wrapped in a burial shroud. It is hidden from view, as Jesus was placed in the tomb. Finally, it is recovered and returned as a representation of the resurrection.

Further, the word afikomen is not Hebrew, it is Greek. It is the only non-Hebrew word in the Passover, and lends credibility to the theory that it was introduced by early believers who spoke Greek. The rabbis believe that the word means "dessert," because it refers to the piece of matzah that is the last thing eaten at the meal. Yet this is not a translation but a consensus. A better translation of the Greek is, "I came!" Jewish Christians see its significance as pointing to Jesus and hope that God will use this to bring more of His people to His Son.

Communion

At this point in the last supper, "Jesus took bread, gave thanks and broke it, and gave it to his disciples, saying, 'Take and eat; this is my body'" (Matthew 26:26).

Although the words were few, the impact and meaning for Christians cannot be overstated. To fully understand this gift of Jesus, we must try to see this moment from the eyes of His disciples. They were at a dinner with Jesus where He had already stated that He would be betrayed by one of them. Now He divides the bread and states that it is His body that they should eat. The disciples might have reasoned, "His body? The only body we eat at Passover is... the Passover lamb!" Jesus was explaining that He was the new Passover lamb. As the original lamb was sacrificed to allow the Jews to be protected from God's wrath in the final plague, so He would be sacrificed to protect us from God's wrath for our sins.

It has been noted that the matzah is a good physical representation of the body of Jesus. In order to comply with the strict rabbinic requirements that the bread not rise at all, it must be pierced so that it has holes, then baked such that it has dark stripes. In the messianic prophecy of Isaiah 53:5, we read, "He was pierced for our transgressions... And with his stripes we are healed."

Further, we read that He blessed the bread before He gave it to the disciples. The wording of this blessing is not given in the Bible, as it was known to all Jews in those times and is known to all Jews even to this day. He would have prayed, "Blessed art Thou, O Lord our God, King of the universe, who brings forth bread from the earth." This can be seen as foreshadowing: Jesus was brought forth from the earth at the resurrection.

We also read that Jesus said, "Do this in remembrance of me" (Luke 22:19). As the entire Passover feast is an occasion of remembrance of the deliverance from Egypt, so should Christians at each communion have a remembrance of their deliverance by Jesus.

After the breaking and giving of the matzah, Jesus "took the cup, gave thanks and offered it to them, saying, 'Drink from it, all of you. This is my blood of the covenant, which is poured out for many for the forgiveness of sins'" (Matthew 26:27-28).

This would have been the third cup of wine, the Cup of Redemption. In Exodus 6:6, God tells the Israelites, "I will redeem you with an outstretched arm." At Passover, this cup is joyfully consumed as recognition that God redeemed the Jews from their slavery to the Egyptians. Jesus specifically used this cup for His Communion, explaining that He was the redeemer from slavery to sin. The blood of the Passover lamb had to be shed to protect the Jews from God's wrath at the tenth plague. So the blood of Jesus, the new Passover lamb, had to be shed to protect us from God's wrath for our sins.

This is the New Covenant, offered to all who believe, that forgiveness of sins comes from the blood of Christ, our Passover lamb.

After the third cup of wine, someone arises and opens the door for Elijah. Elijah was a great prophet of the Jewish Bible. His life is detailed in the books of 1 and 2 Kings. Elijah never physically died; instead, he was taken to heaven in a whirlwind (2 Kings 2:11-12). In Malachi 4:5 we read, "I will send the prophet Elijah before that great and dreadful day of the Lord comes." Based on this prophecy a tradition arose in Judaism that Elijah would return to announce the coming of the Messiah. Furthermore, it was believed that the Messiah would arrive on a Passover. In case Elijah should return, a cup of wine is set out for him at the Passover table. At this point in the service, the door is opened to see if he has indeed returned.

Some time before the last supper, the disciples recognized the divinity of Jesus. They asked, "'Why then do the teachers of the law say that Elijah must come first?' Jesus replied, 'To be sure, Elijah comes and will restore all things. But I tell you, Elijah has already come, and they did not recognize him, but have done to him everything they wished. In the same way the Son of Man is going to suffer at their hands.' Then the disciples understood that he was talking to them about John the Baptist" (Matthew 17:10-13).

In the Gospel of Matthew, we read of Jesus speaking about John the Baptist. He says, "For all the Prophets and the Law prophesied until John. And if you are willing to accept it, he is the Elijah who was to come. He who has ears to hear, let him hear" (Matthew 11:13-15).

On seeing Jesus, and perhaps recognizing His role as the new Passover lamb, John the Baptist said, "Look, the Lamb of God, who takes away the sin of the world!" (John 1:29)

Finally, the Seder concludes with the fourth cup of wine, the Cup of Praise. This last cup is for praising God, the Great Redeemer. With this cup, Psalms and songs of praise are offered. Since ancient times, Psalms 113-118 are sung. These praise Psalms are known as the *Hallel*. The word "hallelujah" is derived from the root word hallel. These would be the hymns sung by Jesus and His disciples before walking to the Garden of Gethsemane.

Before leaving our study of the Passover, it is fascinating to look at the parallels between the Jewish celebration of Passover and the last week of the life of Jesus, known as Passion Week or Holy Week.

PASSOVER	PASSION WEEK	SIGNIFICANCE
A lamb without blemish is brought into each Jewish home four days before the Passover.	Jesus rides into Jerusalem four days before Passover and goes to the Temple.	The unblemished Lamb is in his Father's house four days before the Passover.
To sanctify the Jewish home, a search is carried out for any food made with yeast (symbolic of sin), and it is removed.	Jesus chases the corrupt moneychangers out of the Temple.	Jesus cleanses his Father's house of sin in preparation for Passover.
The special Passover lamb without blemish is sacrificed. The body is eaten.	Jesus shares bread with His disciples, saying, "Take and eat; this is my body."	Jesus is identifying himself as the Passover lamb. Paul says, "For Christ, our Passover lamb, has been sacrificed" (1 Corinthians 5:7).
The blood of the lamb is sprinkled on the doorframes of houses to protect the Jews from God's coming judgment upon the Egyptians, allowing their redemption by God.	Jesus gives communion with the Cup of Redemption. He says, "This is my blood of the covenant, which is poured out for many for the forgiveness of sins" (Matthew 26:26-28). He is crucified less than 24 hours later.	The blood of the Passover lamb brings redemption from the judgment of God.

All the firstborn in Egypt are struck down so that Israel might be freed from physical bondage.	God's firstborn is crucified so that we might be freed from bondage to sin.	Freedom from bondage comes at the cost of the firstborn.

CHAPTER 5 QUESTIONS FOR DISCUSSION

1. The life of Moses, including his Egyptian upbringing and education, prepared him for God's future leadership role. Can you think of circumstances in your own life that molded you according to God's plan for your life?

2. At the Passover, each Jew present is to approach the ceremony as if he had personally been delivered from slavery by God. What could Christians learn about their approach to Communion from this? Does this change the meaning of the words of Jesus, "Do this in remembrance of me"?

3. At the Last Supper, Jesus dressed as a slave to wash the feet of the disciples. Passover is a holiday that celebrates deliverance from slavery. Why do you think Jesus dressed as He did for the washing of the feet?

4. The cup Jesus used to give Communion to His disciples was the Cup of Redemption. The associated words from

Exodus 6:6 state, "I will redeem you with an outstretched arm." What symbolism is here for Christians?

5. In your own words, explain 1 Corinthians 5:6-8.

CHAPTER 6

Using Plagues and Miracles to Overthrow Pagan Gods

The plagues visited upon Egypt (Exodus chapters 7-11) should not be viewed as simply a punishment for those who enslaved God's people. Neither should they be seen purely as a means of bringing humiliation to a tyrant, or a painful means to force him to allow the Hebrews leave Egypt. Although the plagues accomplished these things, there are other points here that should not be missed. First, the plagues were opportunities for repentance. Most were announced in advance, providing Pharaoh with opportunities to repent. Yet he would not admit the error of his ways, and many suffered as a result. Also, the plagues were God's way of overthrowing the gods of Egypt by showing His superiority in their domains. This is revealed in the chart below.

The Ten Plagues	Gods of Egypt Overthrown Before the God of the Jews
1. The Nile river was turned to blood, the fish died, and the river did stink.	The Nile river was worshipped as a god, and there were fish gods as well.
2. Frogs overran the land, getting into beds of the Egyptians, their ovens, and kneading troughs.	Frogs themselves were held sacred, and so could not be killed. Did the Egyptians now appreciate their sacredness?
3. Lice (or gnats) came from "the dust of the ground" and infested the people.	Soil gods could not protect the people. Also, the lice made the priests ceremonially unclean so they could not perform their religious rites.
4. Swarms of flies.	Insects were identified as gods. The fly god was Uatchit. Like the frogs, too much of a good thing!
5. Cattle disease.	Apis, the bull god, shown to be powerless.
6. Moses cast ashes into the air, causing boils on all the people, including the priests.	Priests used ashes to bless the people. Now they were made ill by them. Additionally, the priests were unable to stand before Moses because of the boils.
7. Hail destroyed everything in the fields: people, animals and crops.	Gods of the sky and agriculture shown to be powerless.

8. Locusts ate all that grew back after the hail.	Gods of the fields and grain shown to be powerless.
9. Darkness throughout the land for three days.	Sun god and moon god were banished from heaven.
10. Death of the firstborn.	Pharaoh was himself considered a god, as was his firstborn son, heir to the throne. This son died, showing God's sovereignty over Pharaoh.

The Ten Plagues can be viewed as miracles that proved the superiority of the God of the Jews over the gods of the Egyptians. As a result of this, a number of Egyptians left Egypt with the Hebrews at the Exodus (Exodus 12:38).

Interestingly, some of the miracles of Jesus showed His superiority over the pagan gods of His time. These miracles, witnessed by His disciples, would serve as valuable lessons to them in their future witness to those who worshipped these pagan gods.

PAGAN GOD	ACTION OF JESUS	LESSON
Dionysis: A god of revelry who could allegedly turn water into wine. He also promised life after death, and granted mystical experiences through excessive wine consumption.	Jesus turned water into wine at a wedding feast. (John 2:7-9). He also promised life after death, and granted the mystical experience of receiving the Holy Spirit.	The disciples witnessed Jesus turn water into wine. They could bear witness to seeing Jesus after His death. They could call on the Holy Spirit.

Demitre: A goddess of grain who provided food.	Jesus fed the 5,000 with five loaves and two fish (Matthew 14:15-21). Fed the 4000 with seven loaves and a few fish (Matthew 15:32-38).	Disciples could bear witness to Jesus as a greater provider of food.
Baal: A god who controlled wind, water, rain and storms.	Jesus calms the storm (Matthew 8:23-27). Jesus walks on water (Matthew 14:25).	Disciples witnessed both of these miracles. Could Baal do anything like this?
Aesculapius: A popular god of healing, with a number of temples for healing in Israel, including one uncovered at the Pool of Bethesda.	Jesus heals an invalid who had waited 38 years for healing at the Pool of Bethesda, next to an Aesculapian temple (John 5:1-9).	Who is the greater healer?
Emperors: Shortly after the death of Jesus, Roman emperors started claiming to be gods, and had temples built to themselves.	Jesus was resurrected (Luke 24:36-43). Jesus ascended to heaven (Luke 24:50-51).	Disciples witnessed both of these miracles. Only a true God could undergo resurrection and ascension. Could the emperors do anything like this?

CHAPTER 6 QUESTIONS FOR DISCUSSION

1. Have there been times in your life when prideful resistance to the will of God has led to personal suffering? Did others suffer as well?

2. God used a variety of miracles to show the Egyptians that He was superior to the gods of their lives. Can you think of ways in which God does this today? (Include the "natural miracles" we experience, such as childbirth).

3. What would be your response to the sun and moon disappearing for three days, replaced by total darkness?

4. Which of the ten plagues did God Himself endure later in history?

5. As a result of the ten plagues, a large number of Egyptians left their homes in Egypt to follow the God of the Israelites. How does this parallel the results of the miracles of Jesus?

CHAPTER 7

Elijah and John the Baptist

Elijah is one of the greatest prophets of Israel. His full story is revealed from 1 Kings 17:1 to 2 Kings 8:15. At the end of his life, he did not die but was taken up to heaven in a whirlwind.

There is a key prophecy about Elijah that gives him a prominent place in Judaism even to this day. It is Malachi 4:5: "See, I will send you the prophet Elijah before that great and dreadful day of the Lord comes. He will turn the hearts of the fathers to their children, and the hearts of the children to their fathers; or else I will come and strike the land with a curse." As a result of this prophecy, it is believed that Elijah will return at the end of days to announce the forthcoming arrival of the Messiah. Elijah is seen as Israel's guardian of the Covenant, and is known as the "Angel of the Covenant." He figures prominently in Jewish covenant rituals, including circumcision, the observation of the Sabbath, and the celebration of Passover.

Circumcision is the ritual of bringing a new son into God's covenant with Abraham (Genesis 17:10). It is an honor for the godfather of the boy to hold him during this ceremony. The chair in which the godfather sits is called the Chair of Elijah. The one performing the circumcision, called the *Mohel*, says several prayers. These include, "Elijah, angel of the covenant, see, your own is before you; stand at my right hand and sustain me."

In the traditional celebration of the Sabbath there is a closing ceremony. Elijah is called upon to stand by the family during the week, for protection and to help them in life. One of the closing songs of the Sabbath is also sung at the ending of the Passover Seder, *"Eliyahu ha-navi."* The words of this song are significant: "May the prophet Elijah come soon, in our time, with the Messiah, son of David."

At the celebration of Passover, a cup of wine is set out for Elijah in case he should come to announce the arrival of the Messiah.

Elijah is also important to Christianity. At the Transfiguration, it is Elijah and Moses who appear with Jesus (Mark 9:4). Elijah is here to represent the prophets and their prophecies through the ages. Moses is representing God's laws. Jesus is the fulfillment of both the prophecies and the laws.

Additionally, Elijah is important in the understanding of John the Baptist. When the disciples recognized the divinity of Jesus, they asked, "'Why then do the teachers of the law say that Elijah must come first?' Jesus replied, 'To be sure, Elijah comes and will restore all things. But I tell you, Elijah has already come, and they did not recognize him, but have done to him everything they wished. In the same way the Son of Man is going to suffer at their hands.' Then the disciples understood that he was talking to them about John the Baptist" (Matthew 17:10-13).

John had a concise message: "Repent, for the kingdom of heaven is near" (Matthew 3:2). It was John who had the honor of baptizing Jesus, and it was he who saw the Holy Spirit descend upon Jesus like a dove (Matthew 3:13-17).

Jesus spoke several times about John the Baptist. In Matthew 11:11, He says, "Among those born of women there has not risen anyone greater than John the Baptist." In Matthew 11:13-15, He says, "For all the Prophets and the Law prophesied until John. And if you are willing to accept it, he is the Elijah who was to come. He who has ears to hear, let him hear."

To avoid possible confusion here, it bears stating that John was not a reincarnation of Elijah. Rather, he had the spirit and power of Elijah. This was described by an angel of the Lord to his father, Zechariah, before his birth. He would "go on before the Lord, in the spirit and power of Elijah, to turn the hearts of the fathers to their children and the disobedient to the wisdom of the righteous - to make ready a people prepared for the Lord" (Luke 1:17). This quote certainly harkens to Malachi 4:5.

The book of Mark begins with a prophecy of Isaiah, of which John the Baptist is the fulfillment, "I will send my messenger ahead of you, who will prepare your way - a voice of one calling out in the desert, 'Prepare the way for the Lord, make straight paths for him'" (Mark 1:1-3).

Yet, John the Baptist did not come only to prepare the way for the Lord. As in the traditional belief about Elijah, John also came to announce the coming of the Messiah and a new covenant. He said, "After me will come one more powerful than I, the thongs of whose sandals I am not worthy to stoop down and untie. I baptize you with water, but he will baptize you with the Holy Spirit" (Mark 1:7-8).

CHAPTER 7 QUESTIONS FOR DISCUSSION

1. In all four Gospels, John the Baptist is associated with the words of the prophet Isaiah, "A voice of one calling: In the desert prepare the way for the Lord; make straight in the wilderness a highway for our God." (Isaiah 40:3). What was his message in Matthew 3:2? How did this fulfill the prophecy of Isaiah?

2. What were the differences between the baptisms of John and of Jesus? (John 1:33)

3. How does John announce Jesus when he first recognized Him? (John 1:29)

CHAPTER 8

Jesus Is Our First Fruits

The ancient Jews sought to build their lives around the ever-present awareness that God is One, the source of life, and the provider of all. In deep gratitude and reverence, customs of honoring God with sacrifices and gifts developed from the earliest biblical times. The customs involved presenting to God the first and best of all that He provided, including the firstborn of man, animals and harvest. Some of these offerings were specifically commanded by God and others were voluntary.

In Christianity, we recognize that God also presented to us His first and best: His firstborn Son, created perfectly without blemish.

There are several Biblical lessons concerning offerings to God, which will enhance our understanding of the symbolism of the Jewish feasts. They include the following:

- The offering of the first and best to God begins immediately after Adam and Eve are forced to leave the Garden of Eden for their sin.
- Some sacrifices are favored by God and some are not.
- The offerings and sacrifices were not only given as an expression of thanksgiving but were a statement of faith.
- In addition to being a statement of faith, they also symbolized the faithful expectation of even better things to be provided by God in the future.
- The offerings were in specific cases to be provided as atonement for sin, understood as the substitution of one life for another, provided by the shedding of blood.
- After the Jews were delivered from slavery in Egypt, God claimed the firstborn of all Israel for all time to be His.

To appreciate how early this giving of first fruits and firstborn of the flocks originated, we note in the fourth chapter of Genesis that the sons of Adam and Eve were already offering sacrifices to God. Thus, immediately after Adam and Eve were made to leave the Garden of Eden because of their sin, sacrifices were being offered. One son, Abel, brought to God fat portions (the most valued cut) from the firstborn of his flock. God looked on Abel's offering with favor. However, his brother, Cain, did not bring the first fruits of his harvest, but just "some of the fruits of the soil." The biblical wording here is specific: By not giving the first of the harvest, he was not showing true reverence, and his offering was not looked upon with favor (Genesis 4:3-5).

Later we read that Abraham's faith was tested by God when he was asked to sacrifice his own son, Isaac (Genesis 22:9-12). Abraham proves willing to do this, but God stays the hand of Abraham as he is about to commit the sacrifice. Abraham's willingness was a statement of tremendous faith. He passed the test by revealing that his great faith and reverence for God exceeded his love for his own son.

In Proverbs 3:9-10, we read:

"Honor the Lord with your wealth,

With the first fruits of all your crops;

then your barns will be filled to overflowing,

And your vats will brim over with new wine."

The word "then" is important here. The idea is that the barns will be filled after God is honored with the first fruits. We see the principle of providing the first and best to God as a faithful expectation of better things to be provided by Him in the future.

Sacrifices to atone for sin had to be of animal origin. It was understood that one life, the animal, was being given for another life, that of the one who sinned. We will review this further in the chapter covering the Day of Atonement.

In Exodus 4:22, we read that when Moses returns to Egypt, God tells him to say to Pharaoh, "This is what the Lord says: Israel is my firstborn son." In the process of changing Pharaoh's heart, God sends ten plagues. The last plague was the death of the first-born, including firstborn animals. The Jewish firstborn children and firstborn livestock were protected by the blood of a lamb without blemish being sprinkled over the doorposts of their houses, and God spared those households as He passed over Egypt. In return, God tells the Jews that "the firstborn of every womb among the Israelites belongs to me, whether man or animal" (Exodus13:2). However, although every firstborn child belongs to God, the Bible says that the Jews could redeem the child at the age of one month by paying the priests five silver shekels (Numbers 18:15-16). This allowed the child to live with his family while fulfilling his obligations to God. (We read of the holy family fulfilling this obligation in the second chapter of the book of Luke).

In studying these passages, then looking at the life of Christ, we see that just as man has made sacrifices to God, God has also made sacrifices for us:

- When Adam and Eve sin in the Garden and become aware of their nakedness, God "made garments of skin for Adam and his wife and clothed them" (Exodus 3:21). He must kill an animal for each of them to provide the skin — one life per person.

- When He protected the Hebrews in Egypt from the plague of death of the firstborn, He does this by having each family sacrifice a lamb — one life per family.

- When God gives instructions for how the people should atone for their sins on the Day of Atonement, they are told to sacrifice one lamb for the entire nation.
- When "God so loved the world that he gave his one and only Son, that whoever believes in him shall not perish but have eternal life" (John 3:16), He provided one life for all humankind.

Now having an understanding of the biblical concepts of giving and sacrificing, let us turn to the harvest holiday of First Fruits. This was originally an agricultural holiday, which celebrated the provision of God in bringing forth the barley harvest. Fifteen hundred years before Jesus, God commands that this holy day is to be celebrated on the day after the Sabbath during the week of Passover (Leviticus 23:11).

In modern Judaism, the holiday is minimally celebrated, primarily being recognized as the day to start counting the weeks until the next holiday, *Shavout*, (Pentecost). Yet for Christians, First Fruits is a special day indeed, for it is the holy day commemorating the Resurrection.

Reviewing the last week of the life of Jesus (Holy Week), we note that Jesus was crucified just before the start of the Sabbath of Passover week. He was put into the tomb just before sundown on Friday, which would have ushered in the Sabbath. The Sabbath lasted until sundown Saturday. The tomb was found to be empty

the next morning, Sunday, and Jesus appeared to some of His followers that same day. That day would have been the holy day of
First Fruits. God arranged events so that Jesus was resurrected on
the holy day of First Fruits.

Also, 1,500 years before Jesus walked the earth, God had
commanded specific sacrifices to be offered on the day of First
Fruits (Leviticus 23:12-13). These sacrifices included:

- A lamb without defect
- A grain offering of fine flour mixed with oil
- Wine

The lamb without defect is a New Testament symbol for Jesus.
We note that He is called the "Lamb of God" (John 1:29) and a
"lamb without blemish" (1 Peter 1:19).

The next commanded sacrifice was fine flour mixed with
oil. In the Bible, oil symbolizes anointing, and the name 'Christ'
means, "anointed." Also, note that there is no yeast in the bread,
symbolic of His sinlessness.

Finally, a cup of wine is required, showing the joy of this
sacred event.

So the holy day of First Fruits, commanded by God 1,500
years before the birth of Jesus, became the day of His resurrection.
The sacrifices commanded accurately describe Him. He was our
first fruits: the first to be brought forth from death through His res-

urrection. As the First Fruits of man, He is offered in expectation of a following bountiful harvest of believers.

Paul understood this fully when he wrote: "But Christ has indeed been raised from the dead, the first fruits of those who have fallen asleep. For since death came through a man, the resurrection of the dead comes also through a man. For as in Adam all die, so in Christ all will be made alive. But each in his own turn: Christ, the first fruits; then when he comes, those who belong to him" (1 Corinthians 15:20).

CHAPTER 8 QUESTIONS FOR DISCUSSION

1. What does it mean to be a living sacrifice for God? (Romans 12:1)

2. What has God sacrificed for you? (John 3:16)

3. Why did sacrifices need to be made by the sons of Adam and Eve?

4. Christians believe that salvation is by grace, not by any efforts of men. Yet, in striving to serve God, it is common for Christians to sacrifice their time, money or personal gratification. How can we be sure that such actions are favored, like the sacrifice of Abel, rather than that of

Cain? (Hint: Matthew 5:23-24, Matthew 25:34-40, 2 Corinthians 9:7)

5. Have you "honor[ed] the Lord with your wealth, with the first fruits of all your crops" (Proverbs 3:9-10)? What was the result?

CHAPTER 9

Why the Holy Spirit Was Sent at Pentecost

Pentecost was originally called The Feast of Weeks (Leviticus 23:15-21) because the time of celebration was determined by counting seven full weeks after First Fruits. As this holy day was to commemorate and give thanks for the wheat harvest, which followed the barley harvest, it was also called Latter First Fruits. Modern Jews refer to the holiday by the name of *Shavout*, the Hebrew word for 'weeks.' The date of celebration can also be counted as 50 days after the Sabbath of Passover. In the time of Jesus, the holiday was referred to by the Greek name, Pentecost, meaning "fifty," referring to these 50 days.

Pentecost is very important to Jews. The ancient rabbis determined that this feast occurred at the time Moses reached Mount Sinai, where the Israelites were given the law. Thus, modern Judaism no longer celebrates this as a harvest holiday, but as the time of the giving of the Torah. To honor this giving of God's Law, the books of Exodus 19 and 20 are read in the synagogue on this day.

A review of the events at Mount Sinai helps us understand the significance of this holy day for Christians. God speaks directly to the people in Exodus chapter 20, verbally giving them the Ten Commandments. Then in Exodus 24, Moses leaves the people for 40 days, goes up Mount Sinai, and receives the law written on tablets by God Himself. In Exodus 32, he comes back down the mountain and finds to his horror that the Hebrews are worshipping a golden calf. Moses stands at the entrance to the camp and says, "Whoever is for the Lord, come to me." All those from the tribe of Levi rally to him. He has them take swords and kill many of the idol worshippers, including some who were their own brothers, friends and neighbors. That day "about three thousand" of the people died. Then Moses said, "You have been set apart to the Lord today, for you were against your own sons and brothers, and he has blessed you this day." This was the beginning of the Levite priesthood.

For Christians, Pentecost is the day that commemorates the coming of the Holy Spirit. Leading up to this event, we read in Acts 1 that after the resurrection, Jesus appeared to the disciples and instructed them for 40 days. He then ascended before their eyes. The disciples returned to Jerusalem and stayed there as Jesus had directed.

In Acts 2 the disciples were gathered together on the holy day of Pentecost, probably in one of the patios at the Temple. As Pentecost was a pilgrimage holiday, attendance by Jews from throughout the world was mandated by God 1,500 years beforehand, so "there were staying in Jerusalem God-fearing Jews from every nation under heaven." The Holy Spirit descended upon the disciples, giving them the power to speak in foreign languages. Miraculously, their words were understood by all the Jews present. Peter, filled with the Holy Spirit, makes an uncharacteristically eloquent and persuasive speech, resulting in "about three thousand" who were added to their number. This is the beginning of the Church.

It is fascinating to compare Pentecost at the time of Moses with that at the time of the birth of the Church 1,500 years later:

Pentecost: Moses	Pentecost: Jesus
The people hear God's instruction from Moses.	The disciples hear God's instruction from Jesus.
Moses leaves the Israelites for 40 days to be instructed.	Jesus stays with His followers for 40 days to instruct.
The Jews are gathered at Sinai.	The Jews are gathered in the Temple in Jerusalem.
God descends on Sinai "in fire."	"Tongues as of fire" descend upon the disciples.

God speaks directly to the people, giving them the Ten Commandments.	The Holy Spirit speaks through the disciples to the people, explaining the New Covenant.
God sends the written law with Moses.	The Holy Spirit places the law in the hearts of believers.
A number of Israelites reject God's commands and worship idols.	A number of Israelites repent, recognize their need for a Savior, and accept Jesus.
"About 3000" are killed with the coming of the Law.	"About 3000" are saved with the coming of the Holy Spirit.
The Levites are set apart by being for the Lord.	The disciples are set apart by being for Jesus.
The Levites are blessed by God, becoming God's priesthood on earth for the Covenant of the Law.	The disciples are blessed by the Holy Spirit, becoming God's priesthood on earth for the New Covenant of the Spirit.
The Levites take on the life of caring for the Tabernacle of God, where God would dwell among His people on earth.	The disciples take on the life of caring for the Church of God. God dwells within His people, those who have accepted Christ, as the Holy Spirit.

Pentecost to the Christian is nothing less than the celebration of the coming of the Holy Spirit.

We now compare the required sacrifices for First Fruits (Leviticus 23:12-13) with those of Pentecost (Leviticus 23:16-18). Remembering that God commanded these sacrifices 1,500 years before Jesus, the revealed symbolism is extraordinary. We should also keep in mind that the sacrifices of both holy days were initially to thank God for the harvest of barley (First Fruits), and wheat (Latter First Fruits). Why the remarkable difference in the required sacrifices? For the Christian, the answer is revealed in the symbolism of Christ being our First Fruits, and the believers being the Latter First Fruits.

First Fruits	Latter First Fruits: Pentecost
A lamb without defect.	Seven lambs without defect, two rams.
A grain offering of fine flour mixed with oil.	Two loaves baked with yeast.
Wine.	Wine.

Christ, our First Fruits, is a lamb without blemish.

Believers, the Latter First Fruits, are represented by the seven lambs without defect. The number seven in the Bible refers to perfection or completion of the world (Creation took seven days). The seven lambs are representative of salvation for all the world, or the Church. We, too, become lambs without blemish by the sacrifice of Christ and the coming of the Holy Spirit.

The two rams symbolize that Christ came for both Jew and Gentile (the two groups of people as defined in the Torah).

The grain offering representing Christ is of fine flour mixed with oil, symbolic of anointing. For believers, the bread is made with yeast, symbolizing sin, and reminding us that we are all guilty of sin, requiring a sin substitute. Note that the bread is also in two loaves, again for Jew and Gentile.

The wine reminds us of the joy of knowing Christ has been resurrected as the First Fruits of those who were dead, and the joy we have in belonging to Him.

In 1 Corinthians 15:20-23, we read, "But Christ has indeed been raised from the dead, the first fruits of those who have fallen asleep. For since death came through a man, the resurrection of the dead also comes through a man. For as in Adam all die, so in Christ all will be made alive. But each in his own turn: Christ, the first fruits; then, when He comes, those who belong to Him."

We see a preview of our own future resurrection from death in Matthew 27:52. Here we read, "The tombs broke open and the bodies of many holy people who had died were raised to life. They came out of the tombs, and after Jesus' resurrection they went into the holy city and appeared to many people." These were the first fruits that Jesus offered to God, so that he kept the law even after the Crucifixion. This first fruits offering was made in expectation of the more bountiful harvest to be offered later, when those who belong to Him are brought to God in the final days.

We are those who belong to Him. We are the Latter First Fruits, made acceptable as an offering to God by the coming of the Holy Spirit.

CHAPTER 9 QUESTIONS FOR DISCUSSION

1. The giving of the law at Mt. Sinai can be seen as an elaboration of God's original covenant with Abraham. In Luke 22:20, Jesus spoke of His New Covenant, (see also Jeremiah 31:31). How would you define this New Covenant? What has changed? (Hebrews 9:15)

2. For the Christian, what is the significance of 3,000 dying at the coming of the law, but 3,000 being saved at the coming of the Holy Spirit? (Exodus 32:28; Acts 2:41).

3. Would those around you recognize that you are set apart and blessed? How?

4. At Sinai, the Jews constructed an idol — a false god that they worshipped, thinking it would make their lives better. What idols does our society worship today?

CHAPTER 10

Trumpets: The Return of Christ and the Gathering of Believers

We have reviewed the four feasts that took place in the spring. They symbolize events that have already happened in the mission of Christ:

- At Passover, He gave us Communion and was crucified.
- On the Feast of Unleavened Bread, He was placed in the tomb.
- On First Fruits, He was resurrected.
- At Pentecost, He sent the Holy Spirit to us.

We now turn to the three fall feasts. These symbolize events that are to be fulfilled on His return:

- The Feast of Trumpets represents the return of Christ and the gathering of believers.

- The Day of Atonement will mark the final Day of Judgment.
- The Feast of Tabernacles marks the return of Christ to dwell with us again.

The first of the three fall feasts is the Feast of Trumpets. It is a day for the Jewish people to gather together. This season is so holy to the Jews that they consider it the beginning of the year, even though it occurs during the seventh month. (This distinction of being the beginning of the year is not necessarily biblical, but probably arose from traditions observed at the time of the Babylonian captivity. Jews today call the holiday *Rosh Hashanah*, which means "head of the year.") The Feast of Trumpets begins a holy season that to the Jewish mind can be compared to a legal trial. The trial begins with evidence of sinful acts being presented through self-evaluation on the Feast of Trumpets. This is followed by pleading for mercy during the ensuing ten days of repentance. Finally, judgment is received on the Day of Atonement, with the hoped-for result being a full return to God.

The Feast of Trumpets is described in Leviticus 23:23, when the Jews are told that the day is to be observed by abstaining from work and holding a sacred assembly. The day is to be commemorated by over one hundred blasts on a trumpet.

Trumpets are significant throughout the Bible. The Hebrew word for trumpet is *shofar*. A shofar is made from the horn of a ram. In addition to heralding the Feast of Trumpets, there are numerous other occasions when a shofar is used in the Bible:

- At the coronation of an earthly king (1 Kings 1:34, 39).
- Announcing the presence of God as King (Psalm 47:5).
- At the giving of the Law (Exodus 19:13, 19).
- As a warning alarm to the people (Amos 3:6).
- As a signal to gather troops for battle (Judges 3:27).
- As a force to bring down the walls of Jericho (Joshua 6).
- To herald the Messianic Age and the Day of Judgment (Isaiah 27:13).

Additionally, the shofar has significance to the Jews because it must be made from the horn of a ram and not any other animal. We remember the story of the test of Abraham when he is asked to sacrifice his only son, Isaac. Just as he is about to do so, God stays his hand. Instead of being required to sacrifice Isaac, God provides a substitution in the form of a ram caught in a nearby bush. This ram is caught in the bush *by his horns*. The story illustrates the concept of substitutionary atonement: God provides a life to substitute for the one that was called to be sacrificed. This idea is the basis for sacrificing animals for the sins of Israel, which figured so prominently in the ritual worship of ancient Judaism. Christians recognize this concept in the sacrifice of Jesus for the sins of man.

Modern observances of this holiday include attending the synagogue for services in the evening and again for the entire following day. The mood is somber yet hopeful. It is a time for Jews to gather together in spiritual preparation and repentance. As the Jews take stock of their spiritual condition, they consider changes that need to be made. It is of great importance to try to resolve any grievances during this time, as God wishes us all to dwell together as brothers. Forgiveness of those who have caused offense is emphasized, as the Jews anticipate asking God to forgive their offenses against Him. Jesus certainly would approve of this emphasis on making amends, as He reminds us when He says in Matthew 5:23-24, "Therefore, if you are offering your gift at the altar and there remember that your brother has something against you, leave your gift there in front of the altar. First go and be reconciled to your brother; then come and offer your gift."

The emphasis of the holy season is not on judgment, but rather on averting judgment through repentance and asking God for mercy. Jews recognize that sin is inevitable, for absolute sinlessness is a trait of God alone. Therefore, repentance and seeking mercy are essential in returning to God.

Three themes mark the feast of Trumpets:

- God's sovereignty.
- Remembrance of the covenant between Israel and God: that God has always been faithful to Israel, although Israel has not always been faithful to God.

- The sounds of the shofar. To the Jewish mind, the sounds of the shofar represent Israel's repentance, God's judgment, and divine restoration.

There is great Christian symbolism found in the sounding of the shofar as well. A number of scriptures mention the blowing of the trumpet to herald the Messianic Age and the Day of Judgment.

In the prophesy of Isaiah 27:13, we read, "In that day the Lord will thresh from the flowing Euphrates to the Wadi of Egypt, and you, O Israelites, will be gathered up one by one. And in that day a great trumpet will sound."

In Matthew 24:30-31, Jesus tells the disciples that, "At that time the sign of the Son of Man will appear in the sky, and all the nations of the earth will mourn. They will see the Son of Man coming on the clouds of the sky, with power and great glory. And he will send his angels with a loud trumpet call, and they will gather his elect from the four winds, from one end of the heavens to the other."

In his writings, Paul elaborates on the return of Jesus to claim His followers. In 1 Corinthians 15:51-52 we find, "Listen, I tell you a mystery: We will not all sleep, but we will all be changed - in a flash, in the twinkling of an eye, at the last trumpet. For the trumpet will sound, the dead will be raised imperishable, and we will be changed." In 1 Thessalonians 4:16, he writes, "For the Lord himself will come down from heaven, with a loud command, with the voice of the archangel and with the trumpet call of God, and the dead in Christ will rise first."

Trumpets also are important in the final days described in the book of Revelation. In Revelation 8:2, we read of seven angels who are given seven trumpets. In Revelation 11:15, "The seventh angel sounded his trumpet, and there were loud voices in heaven, which said: 'The kingdom of the world has become the kingdom of our Lord and of his Christ, and he will reign for ever and ever.'"

The trumpet of ancient Israel heralded an ingathering of the Jews for a time of repentance, followed by a day of judgment and a hoped-for atonement. This foreshadows the return of Christ to earth, when a trumpet will announce His return and herald an ingathering of believers. This will be followed by a time of repentance for the non-believing world, followed by a day of final judgment and, it is hoped, atonement for many.

CHAPTER 10 QUESTIONS FOR DISCUSSION

1. The Feast of Trumpets ushers in a time of God's judgment. Are Christians judged? Read Romans 14:10-12. What is the difference between believers and non-believers when God judges? See also Hebrews 7:25.

2. The Feast of Trumpets is also the beginning of a period marked by reconciliation with others. Do you have a rela-

tionship that needs reconciliation? Considering the words of Jesus in Matthew 5:23-24, what action could you take to improve that relationship?

3. Read the words of Jesus in Matthew 24:30-31. If you knew that the trumpet He spoke about would blow one week from today, what would you do differently?

CHAPTER 11

Atonement by Blood

A fter the Feast of Trumpets and the ten-day period of repentance comes the Day of Atonement, also called *Yom Kippur*. In ancient Israel, atonement could only come through making a sacrifice involving blood. This was based on the instruction given in Leviticus 17:11: "For the life of a creature is in the blood, and I have given it to you to make atonement for yourselves on the altar; it is the blood that makes atonement for one's life." On the Day of Atonement, all Israel looked to the high priest to make sacrifices for the atonement of the nation. This concept is readily understood by Christians, who believe that Jesus had to shed blood for us to have atonement with God.

The sacrifices on the Day of Atonement were first performed in the ancient Tabernacle, then continued in the Temple in Jerusalem. These rituals were still being practiced in the time of Jesus. Yet after the Temple was destroyed in 70 A.D., the Jews were left without an acceptable place to perform their sacrifices. This was not without precedent for them, as the same situation presented during the Babylonian captivity after the destruction of the Temple of Solomon in 586 B.C. Following the example of the exiled prophet Daniel (Daniel 6:10), prayer replaced blood sacrifice as the primary means of achieving atonement. To this day, Jews observe the Day of Atonement by spending the day at the synagogue in fervent prayer. The prayer is complemented by fasting. It is believed that judgment will come at the end of this day, with the decision of whether each person is inscribed for another year into the Book of Life. The service closes with a final blowing of the shofar.

This is remarkably different than the way in which the rituals were observed before the destruction of the Temple. So important were these rituals that the entire sixteenth chapter of Leviticus was devoted to describing them. Nothing less than the atonement of the nation of Israel was at stake. This was the only day of the year in which the high priest could present himself directly before the presence of God in the inner sanctuary of the Tabernacle, called the Holy of Holies.

The Atonement rituals included several steps:

- The high priest washed himself, then dressed in sacred linen clothing.
- He sacrificed a bull for himself and his household. Blood from the bull was carried into the sacred place where God

dwelled and judged man, the Holy of Holies, where it was sprinkled seven times on the atonement cover of the Ark of the Covenant.

- Then two male goats without blemish were selected. By casting lots, one was determined to be sacrificed and the other to be a scapegoat.

- The first goat was sacrificed. Its blood was carried by the high priest into the Holy of Holies. There the blood was sprinkled on the atonement cover and other places in the Tabernacle. This was to "make atonement for the most holy place because of the uncleanness and rebellion of the Israelites, whatever their sins have been" (Leviticus 16:16).

- Returning to the courtyard of the Tabernacle, the high priest then placed his hands on the head of the second goat. This was to "confess over it all the wickedness and rebellion of the Israelites - all their sins - and put them on the goat's head" (Leviticus 16:21). The goat was then carried far away into the wilderness and released. This served to take the sins of the Israelites far away from them.

For Christians, Jesus served as both of the goats sacrificed for the sins of the people. As the first goat, He was sacrificed at His crucifixion. Paul summarizes this belief in Romans 3:23-25: "For all have fallen short of the glory of God, and are justified freely by his grace through the redemption that came by Christ Jesus. God presented him as a sacrifice of atonement, through faith in his blood."

As the second goat, He served to let all of us place our hands on Him through our belief in His sacrifice. Then He carried our sins far away from us.

In heaven is the true Tabernacle set up by the Lord, (Hebrews 8:2, Revelation 15:5) after which the earthly Tabernacle was patterned. After the Resurrection, it was to this heavenly tabernacle that Jesus carried His own blood. There He entered the true Holy of Holies to offer it for our atonement before God. This is described in Hebrews 9:11: "When Christ came as high priest of the good things that are already here, he went through the greater and more perfect tabernacle that is not man-made, that is to say, not a part of this creation. He did not enter by means of the blood of goats and calves; but he entered the Most Holy Place once for all by His own blood, having obtained eternal redemption." (For further biblical elaboration on these points, the reader is encouraged to read Hebrews chapters 8-10.)

As the Day of Atonement represents the most holy day of the year for the Jews, so it also represents the most holy concept of Christianity: Jesus sacrificed for our sins to make atonement for us with God.

CHAPTER 11 QUESTIONS FOR DISCUSSION

1. Why do you think the high priest had to offer a blood sacrifice for himself before making a blood sacrifice for the Israelites? Would Jesus have to do this? Why? See Hebrews 7:27-28, 9:12.

2. Whose blood is used to make an atonement sacrifice for Christians (Matthew 26:28)?

3. At the time of the Tabernacle, for how long a period of time did the blood sacrifice provide atonement?

4. How long does the blood sacrifice, made by Jesus on behalf of believers, provide atonement (John 3:16; Hebrews 10:13-14)?

CHAPTER 12

Dwelling with God:
The Feast of Tabernacles

The Feast of Tabernacles is an eight-day festival that has been celebrated by the Jews from the time it was commanded by God through Moses (Leviticus 23:33-44). On the first day there was to be a sacred assembly of all the Jews and no work was to be done. For the next seven days, the Israelites were commanded to live in temporary shelters called *sukkahs*. The sukkahs remind the Jews of the years after enslavement in Egypt, when they wandered in the wilderness. In those days, as God provided for them He also dwelt among them, living in the Tabernacle as they camped around it in their tents.

This was an agricultural holiday as well as a holiday of thanksgiving. It came at the completion of the hard work of harvesting the grain and the gathering and pressing of the olives and grapes. At the time of Jesus, it was celebrated by tens of thousands in

Jerusalem, as it was one of the pilgrimage feasts. The city would have been surrounded by hundreds of the sukkahs, and it would have been a very joyous, exciting and crowded time.

As it was an agricultural holiday, a ritual of petitioning God for the winter rains developed. These early seasonal rains were called the "former rains," and were vital to the crops and livestock. Each morning of the festival, a procession of priests would gather in the Temple. Trumpets were blown and great crowds would assemble to watch. The priests would walk to the Pool of Siloam and fill a gold pitcher with water. Then they would solemnly return and ceremoniously pour out the water upon the altar, as a request to God that He send the essential early rains.

At the time of Jesus, another ritual was observed during the Feast of Tabernacles, which involved the lighting of the lamps. In the Temple courtyard and on the walls were a number of very large golden lampstands. Each of these had gold cups filled with oil. At dusk they were lit and the combined light was so great that the illumination could be seen throughout Jerusalem. The light harkened to the Shekinah glory of God dwelling among the Israelites.

In modern Judaism, the Feast of Tabernacles (called *Sukkoth* by the Jews) is celebrated throughout the world. During the holiday, Jews may live in or eat meals in the outdoor booths assembled specifically for the holiday observance. Some families build their own sukkah, and some synagogues build a large one for the entire congregation to enjoy. In Israel, these can be seen even on apartment balconies during this time. While there are no instructions for how the walls of the booth are to be put together, the roof must be made of something that grows from the ground (branches, bamboo, leaves, boards) and must allow enough sky to be visible so that stars can be seen.

The actual word for tabernacle comes from the Greek *skene*, which means "tent or dwelling place." This concept of God dwelling with man is essential to both Judaism and Christianity. God dwelt among the Israelites as they wandered in the wilderness, revealing Himself as the Shekinah glory, and communicating directly with Moses in the Tabernacle.

Christians believe that God has tabernacled with man in three ways:

- As the Father Himself, the Shekinah glory, in ancient Israel.
- As the Son of Man, Jesus Christ, incarnate as a man (Matthew 16:15-17, John 10:30, John 12:45).
- As the Holy Spirit, living in the hearts of believers (John 14:17, 1 Corinthians 6:19).

At a Feast of Tabernacles 2,000 years ago, Jesus chose to announce His position as the provider of the Holy Spirit to those who believe, whereby God would dwell within the bodies of man. Twice during that feast He told listeners that His teachings were from God and that God had sent Him (John 7:16-17, 28-29). Then He went on to say that He Himself was the source of the Holy Spirit, which He described as living water: "On the last and greatest day of the Feast, Jesus stood and said in a loud voice, 'If anyone is thirsty, let him come to me and drink. Whoever believes in me, as the Scripture has said, streams of living water will flow from within him.' By this He meant the Spirit, whom those who believed in him were later to receive" (John 7:37-39).

Remembering that earlier in the day the crowds would have watched the priests pour out water on the altar, Jesus was making an analogy for those present. As the people turned to God for the rain vital to their physical life, so they should turn to Him for the Holy Spirit, which was vital to their spiritual life, and indeed eternal life. Whoever believed in Him would receive streams of living water, the Holy Spirit.

Jesus also employed the symbolism of the lighting of the lamp-stands in the Temple to explain Himself. Shortly after the feast, Jesus stated, "I am the light of the world. Whoever follows me will never walk in darkness, but will have the light of life" (John 8:12). As the lighting of the lampstands symbolized the Shekinah glory of God, so did Jesus claim to be God's light on earth, the "light of the world." Furthermore, we read in Matthew 5:14 that Jesus tells His followers, "You are the light of the world." Believers in Jesus become the light of the world by reflecting the light that comes from Him through having the Holy Spirit.

CHAPTER 12 QUESTIONS FOR DISCUSSION

1. The Feast of Tabernacles celebrates God's provision. Beginning from your youth, in what ways has God provided for you? Reviewing your life, are there times when you now recognize His provision that were not apparent at the time? What lesson can you learn from this?

2. In the wilderness, God dwelled among the Jews in a way that was apparent. When Jesus dwelled among His disciples, He was also apparent. How is God apparent to us today? Have you personally experienced the presence of God? In what way?

3. Why do you think Jesus picked this holy day to declare, "Whoever believes in me, as the scripture has said, streams of living water will flow from within him" (John 7:37-39)?

4. What are some ways in which those who believe in Jesus are the light of the world? (John 7:37-39)

CHAPTER 13

Jesus in the Ancient Tabernacle

∩

Shortly after being delivered from slavery in Egypt, the Jews were given meticulous instructions for building a structure that would serve as a place for God to dwell among them (Exodus 25-31). This was the holy Tabernacle. It would also serve as the place to make sacrifices to God so that His people might receive atonement for their sins. The importance of this structure can be appreciated by noting that while only two chapters of the Bible are devoted to describing the creation of the universe, over 50 involve the design and ceremonies of the Tabernacle. The design of the Tabernacle was used in constructing the Temple of Solomon and the later, expanded Temple mentioned throughout the New Testament. The Tabernacle is an astonishing and perfect representation of God and His desire to dwell with and enjoy us, even as we have the blessed privilege to dwell with and enjoy Him.

We will see that it also is richly symbolic of the Christian life and Christ Himself.

It is nothing short of miraculous that such a structure could be built in the midst of the desert. The amount of metals and fabric required was tremendous, and it all was brought out of Egypt. Several points bear mentioning here.

We know from ancient Scripture that the Jews were employed in building cities for Pharaoh while they were slaves in Egypt. It was during this time that they acquired skill in molding gold, silver and bronze. Additionally, they would have learned to work with curtains and fabric.

The source of the materials is revealed in Exodus. We read that after the tenth plague, the Jews were allowed to leave Egypt. As they were on their way out, they "did as Moses instructed and asked the Egyptians for articles of silver and gold and for clothing. The Lord had made the Egyptians favorably disposed toward the people, and they gave them what they asked for; so they plundered the Egyptians" (Exodus 12:35). Hence, the Jews left Egypt with a great cache of precious metals and fabric.

The Tabernacle was ingeniously designed for portability. The entire structure could be disassembled and hand carried by its component parts. All of the furnishings had rings through which poles were placed, and these poles were used for lifting and transporting. This is all the more amazing when the weight of the component poles and furnishings is considered. It is estimated that the assembled structure contained over three tons of silver, over two tons of bronze and one ton of gold!

We will refer to the following diagram as we describe the fascinating structure of the Tabernacle.

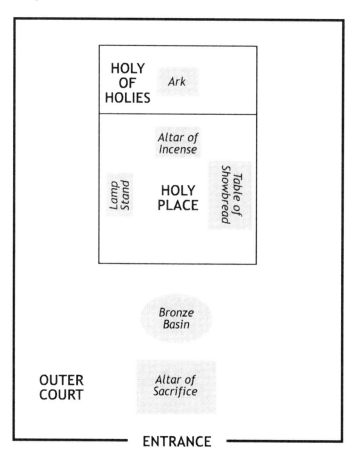

ENTRANCE

The Tabernacle

The outer courtyard of the Tabernacle was 150 feet long and 75 feet wide. The courtyard was framed by a perimeter curtain made of fine linen suspended by a series of poles. This curtain was 7½ feet tall. The courtyard was entered through this curtain at the east end.

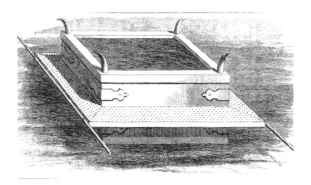

The Bronze Altar

As one entered, the first object encountered was a bronze altar which was 7½ feet long, 7½ feet wide and 4½ feet high. It was here that animals were sacrificed for the sins of the people. The person bringing the offering would place his hand on the head of the animal while it was being killed to signify that the animal was actually a substitute. Christians believe that a blood sacrifice is required for atonement for sins, and that the sacrifice of Jesus on the Cross fulfilled this function for all who believe in Him.

As we will see in all of the furnishings of the Tabernacle, the materials used have symbolic value. In this case we note that the altar was made of bronze. Bronze is a mixed, impure metal (as opposed to gold, which is pure). Bronze therefore represents the things of man.

The Bronze Laver

Beyond the bronze altar was a bronze laver made from mirrors that were donated by the women of Israel (Exodus 38:8). The laver was a large bowl containing water for ceremonial washing after the sacrifices had been made. The priest was commanded to wash his hands and feet after the sacrifice so that he would be cleansed before entering the Tent of Meeting. If he did not wash, he might die upon entering (Exodus 30:20). This washing symbolizes baptism for the Christian, as well as the receiving of the Holy Spirit. That the laver was made by melting down mirrors is noteworthy. Mirrors are a symbol of pride and reflect our imperfections. It is the overcoming of our pride that allows us to recognize we will never be righteous enough to enter a perfect heaven of our own accord, but need a divine mediator.

The Tent of Meeting

Beyond the laver was the Tent of Meeting, so named because it was the location where Moses would meet directly with God. The tent measured 45 feet long, 15 feet wide and 15 feet high.

The tent was entered from the east through a curtain, and a second curtain partitioned the front 30-foot section from the back 15-foot section.

The covering consisted of four layers of fabric. The innermost layer was of fine linen, made of blue, purple and scarlet fibers. Immediately over this were two layers of goatskin. The inner goatskin layer was not dyed, but the outer was dyed red. Over the outer goatskin layer was a layer of sea cow skin. The skin would have served to protect the other layers and was water repellant.

Christians can see Jesus represented in all four of these layers. Beginning at the innermost layer, we find it was made of fine linen, which stands for righteousness (Revelation 19:8). It was woven with blue, purple and scarlet fibers; each if these colors had symbolism for the Jews. The color blue symbolized heaven; purple was the color of royalty; and scarlet was the color of blood. All of this is found in Jesus. In Him we find righteousness. He came from heaven and returned to heaven. He is the royal King of kings. He shed His blood for our sins.

In the next two layers we also find Jesus. These are the two layers of goatskin, with the outermost layer dyed red. These layers hearken back to the ritual sacrifices of the Day of Atonement. We remember that one goat becomes a blood sacrifice (goatskin dyed red) and another was designated as the scapegoat. For believers, Christ serves as both goats. He was our substitute blood sacrifice on the Cross, and also our scapegoat as He takes our sins far away from us.

The outermost layer of the Tent of Meeting would have been plain, ordinary leather. This covering reminds us that Jesus Himself appeared as a plain and ordinary man on the outside. Yet, inside the Tent was the beautiful glory of God, and so it was with Jesus, who was also truly God.

The front section of the Tent of Meeting was known as the Holy Place. Here were three pieces of furniture: the Table of Shewbread, which held 12 loaves of bread; a seven-branched lampstand; and an altar for burning incense. In the Tent of Meeting, all furnishings were either pure gold or wood covered in gold. Gold is a pure metal and represented God. Wood, being perishable, symbolized man. The wooden objects covered in gold symbolized man in the presence of God.

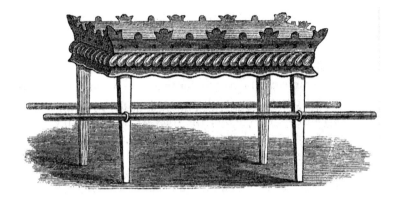

The Table of Shewbread

The Table of Shewbread was 3 feet long, 1½ feet wide and 2¼ feet tall. It was made of wood covered with gold. Once a week on the Sabbath, each of the 12 tribes supplied a loaf of bread made from finely milled flour. All 12 loaves were placed on the Table. The bread symbolized the everlasting Covenant between God and the Israelites, as each tribe was represented in God's Holy Place. The bread also served as a reminder of God's provision. The priests were allowed to eat this bread at the end of the week (Exodus 25:23-30).

As the bread symbolized the everlasting covenant between God and the Israelites, so for Christians it symbolizes our everlasting covenant with God through Christ. To the Jews the bread also served as a reminder of God's sustenance, and so it serves for us. Additionally, the loaves represent that which we bring to God: worship, praise, love, service, and tithes or other offerings.

The Golden Lampstand

The golden Lampstand had seven branches, and was hammered from a single piece of pure gold. It held oil lamps, and was the only source of light in the otherwise dark Tent of Meeting (Exodus 25:31-40).

For the Christian, this Lampstand symbolizes Jesus Himself. In the seven branches we see a symbol of the world and its creation in seven days. Jesus came to save the world. The oil in the lamps reminds us of the oil of anointing, and the name Christ means "The Anointed One." The light reminds us that Jesus said, "I am the light of the world. Whoever follows me will never walk in darkness, but will have the light of life" (John 8:12). In following Jesus, the Christian can be illumined with the divine light of life.

The Altar of Incense

The Altar of Incense was 1½ feet wide, 1½ feet long and 3 feet tall. It was made of wood and covered with gold. Incense of a prescribed formula was burned constantly on the altar, representing man communicating with God through prayer. The burning incense represents the prayers of man ascending to God

(Revelation 8:3-4). Christians can here see Jesus praying for us and intervening for us with God continually (Hebrews 7:25).

The back section of the Tent of Meeting was known as the Most Holy Place. In it were two pieces of furniture: the Ark of the Covenant and the Mercy Seat.

The Ark of the Covenant

The Ark of the Covenant was 2¼ feet wide, 3¾ feet long and 2¼ feet high. It was made of wood and overlaid with gold. The Ark contained the tablets of the law given to Moses by God on Mt. Sinai. The Ark also contained a gold jar of manna to remind the Israelites of God's provision in the wilderness. Finally, it contained Aaron's staff that budded (Numbers 17:8), to remind all Israel that Aaron and his descendants were chosen by God to be the high priests (Exodus 25:10-22).

For Christians, all three of these have special significance. The tablets of the law represent the law that is placed in our minds and hearts when we receive the Holy Spirit (Hebrews 8:10). The gold jar containing manna served as a reminder of God's provision for the Hebrews in the wilderness, and so it assures Christians that God provides for us today if we seek first His kingdom and His righteousness (Matthew 6:31-33). Aaron's staff, a dead stick of wood that budded and produced fruit (Numbers 17:8) reminds Christians of the resurrection and the promise of being raised to eternal life (1 Corinthians 15:52).

Topping the Ark was the Mercy Seat, also known as the "atonement cover." It was made entirely of gold and consisted of a platform that also served as the top lid of the Ark. At each end were cherubim kneeling with their wings extended toward each other. These wings formed the Mercy Seat on which God sat to judge His people. It is here that God would sit to judge the Hebrews.

Christians believe that Jesus sits at the right hand of God and has the authority to judge men (John 5:27), and believe they are sanctified by His sacrifice at Crucifixion.

Reviewing the Tabernacle as a whole, we note that it contained three veils, which functioned as doors of entry. The first

veil served as an entryway from the outer world into the court-
yard. The second opened into the front of the Tent of Meeting, the
Holy Place. The third was the veil between the Holy Place and the
Most Holy Place.

In the three veils of the Tabernacle we find Jesus again. Like
the innermost layer of the Tent, these veils were all made of fine
linen and were woven with threads of blue, purple and scarlet.

- The first veil divided the courtyard from the outside world.
  It signified leaving the realm of the world and voluntarily
  moving closer to God. It thus opened the way to God.
- The second veil divided the outer courtyard from the
  Holy Place of God. This veil, then, opened to the realm
  of directly interacting with God through prayer (the Altar
  of Incense), His Covenant (Table of Shewbread), and His
  illumination (the Lampstand). This realm brings man to
  the truth.
- The third veil divided the Holy Place from the Most Holy
  Place. It opened directly into God's realm of everlasting
  life.

Thus, the three veils give symbolic meaning to the statement
of Jesus: "I am the way and the truth and the life. No one comes to
the Father except through me" (John 14:6).

The Most Holy Place was the realm of God, separated from the rest of the Tabernacle by the third curtain. No one except the high priest could enter this area, and even he could enter only once a year behind a thick cloud of incense. Remembering that the Temple in Jerusalem was modeled after the Tabernacle, this veil was the one torn at the moment of the death of Christ (Matthew 27:51). It represents His body being torn to give His followers direct access to God.

The Tabernacle as a Model of the Christian Gospel

The word *gospel* means "good news." The Christian Gospel message is presented in the New Testament. It can be viewed as consisting of four specific truths, all of which are found represented in the Tabernacle.

The first truth is about God: that He is the holy creator of everything, including man. To Him we owe our very existence, as well as our continued sustenance. Therefore, we are absolutely dependent on Him, and He has an absolute claim on us (Acts 17: 24-25). We were created by God to worship Him and serve Him (Matthew 4:10). The first gospel truth, then, is: We are absolutely dependent on God, and He has every right to ask us to live according to His standards.

In the Tabernacle, we see a structure specifically designed by God for man, the purpose of which is to allow for man to worship and serve God in His specified way.

The second truth of the Christian gospel is about man's nature. Christians believe that man is inherently sinful, meaning that every man will fall short of perfect and righteous behavior over time. As God is perfect, and we are not, we are in a situation where we are separated from Him. To be seen by God as perfect and righteous, we need some means of reconciliation. The second truth can be summarized as: Our imperfect nature separates us from our perfect God, creating a need for a means of reconciliation. At the Tabernacle, we find the perfect God dwelling in the presence of the imperfect Hebrews. A means of reconciliation was needed, and God provided this through a system of ceremonial sacrifices. The blood of the sacrifices allowed for man to receive atonement from God for imperfect, unrighteous behavior (Leviticus 17: 11).

The third gospel truth concerns Jesus. The Bible teaches that Jesus, through His blood sacrifice at crucifixion, has provided the means for atonement for all men. The third Christian gospel truth is: Jesus has provided the only way for imperfect, unrighteous man to be reconciled to his Creator God.

We note that in entering the Tabernacle, the first piece of furniture encountered is the altar of sacrifice. This reveals that the first step in approaching God requires being reconciled to Him by making a blood sacrifice. In Christianity, the first step in approaching God is by an acceptance on faith that Jesus allowed His own blood to be shed (John 10:14-18) that we might be reconciled to God. It is His blood sacrifice that makes us acceptable to God, in spite of our imperfect, unrighteous nature.

The fourth Christian gospel truth is: As God has provided a means for all men to be reconciled to Him by providing His own son as our blood sacrifice (John 3:16), it is reasonable for God to expect us to place our faith in Christ and turn our lives around, (repent), in service to Him.

In the Tabernacle, just past the Altar of Sacrifice, was the Bronze Laver, a basin of water in which the priests would wash before approaching the holy place of God. After becoming a follower of Christ by accepting His blood sacrifice on the cross, Christians are baptized, symbolizing that they are now cleansed of their previous secular lives, and now may enter a life of serving God.

Beyond the Bronze Laver was the Holy Place, in which we find symbolism relating to a life of worshipping and living for God. Entering here, we find the Table of the Shewbread, representing the presence of each of the twelve tribes before God. In the same way, the Christian is constantly in God's presence because of his relationship with Christ, who sits at the right hand of God. Also in the Holy Place is the Lampstand, symbolic of the light of Christ. Christians have access to this through the Holy Spirit. The third fixture here is the Altar of Incense, representing our prayers going up to God. Christians have the blessed privilege of praying directly to God, represented by this altar.

At the death of Christ on the cross, the curtain in the Temple in Jerusalem was torn from top to bottom (Matthew 27:51). Remembering that the Temple was modeled after the Tabernacle, this would have been the curtain between the Holy Place and the Most Holy Place. The symbolism is that the sacrifice of Jesus allows us direct access to the holy realm of God. The curtain was torn from top to bottom to show that God had performed this. If man had torn the curtain, it would have been torn from bottom to top.

The Most Holy Place continues in rich Christian symbolism. Here was the Ark of the Covenant, containing a golden container of manna, showing that God will continue to provide for his people. Also in the Ark was the staff that budded, symbolizing the granting of eternal life through Resurrection. In addition, in the Ark were the stone tablets on which the Commandments were written. For the Christian, these Commandments are written on our hearts when we receive the Holy Spirit (Hebrew 10:16).

Finally, the Most Holy Place contained the Mercy Seat, where God sat in judgment of Israel. The Bible says much about God's judgment, but Christians are assured that in Jesus they have a high priest who pleads for them before God, and is able to "save completely those who come to God through him, because he always lives to intercede for them." (Hebrews 7:25)

CHAPTER 13 QUESTIONS FOR DISCUSSION

1. Look up the definition of "atonement." In ancient times, the Jews made atonement with God by the blood sacrifice of animals. How do Christians receive atonement today?

2. The high priests serving in the Tabernacle had to wash before entering God's Holy Place. How are Christians prepared to enter God's Holy Place today?

3. Read Matthew 27:51. The curtain that was torn functioned to separate the Holy Place from the Most Holy Place. What is the symbolism in the tearing of the curtain for the Christian? What does it mean to you personally?

4. The altar of incense represents the prayers of men ascending to God, who hopefully will find them to be a pleasing aroma. Do you pray daily? Do you approach God in humility? Do you approach God in reverence?

CHAPTER 14

Christ and His Bride: Ancient Jewish Wedding Customs

The Gospels and the Letters of Paul contain numerous parables and lessons relating to Jewish wedding customs at the time of Jesus. Understanding the customs of this joyous occasion brings us a deeper understanding of many of the teachings of Jesus and the explanations of Paul. The groom-bride relationship itself reflects the relationship of Jesus with His followers, as we read in Ephesians 5:31: "For this reason a man will leave his father and mother and be united to his wife, and the two will become one flesh. This is a profound mystery — but I am talking about Christ and the church."

Studying the Jewish wedding customs of biblical times greatly enhances our understanding of our relationship with Christ and our duties to Him as His bride.

In the Jewish tradition, there were three stages in becoming married: the contractual agreement, the betrothal, and the wedding celebration itself.

The Contractual Agreement

First, of course, a bride had to be selected. It was common for the father of the groom to select a bride for his son, sometimes while the boy was still an infant. If it were very impractical for the father himself to do this, he could delegate a representative. In Genesis 24, we find Abraham sending his servant to find a wife for Isaac because Abraham was then very old. As Israel's population grew, being a professional matchmaker became a way to make a living.

When the bride was found, the two family patriarchs would meet (without the children or wives present) and negotiate a contract. A dowry would be discussed which would be paid by the groom's family, and the dowry could be quite expensive for families of means. The cost in today's dollars could be as much as a new home! Thus, the bride was actually being bought with a price.

When agreement was reached, both families would meet for the writing and signing of the marriage contract (*Ketubah*). It included provisions and conditions proposed for the marriage, including the groom's promise to support and take care of his wife-to-be. For the bride's part, the contract would state her financial status and what possessions of significance she would be bringing to the marriage. The bride did have the right to decline the offer.

The Betrothal

The signing would be followed by a ceremony. To prepare for the ceremony, the bride and groom would separately have a ritual immersion in a water bath (*mikveh*). This was symbolic of spiritual cleansing. Afterwards, the couple appeared under the wedding canopy (*huppah*) to publicly express their intention to become engaged. The wedding canopy represented the new household being planned. At the end of the ceremony, the vows were sealed with a cup of wine.

The wedding would not be held for about a year; however, the couple was now considered as married before the world, and this was very binding. To break up at this point would actually require a religious divorce, and this remedy was only available to the husband. Once the bride accepted the contract, she could not withdraw from it.

The year before the wedding was a time for sanctification and purification. The couple lived apart during this time and there were no sexual relations until the wedding celebration.

Both bride and groom had duties and responsibilities during the betrothal period. The bride would wear a veil whenever she went out so that eligible young men would know she was not available. Purity and modesty were emphasized. She would use this time to sew her wedding clothes, prepare for marriage and be reflective.

It is instructive to Christians to note that this is the period of betrothal in which Mary revealed to Joseph that she was pregnant. Joseph planned to obtain a religious divorce, but an angel of the Lord appeared to him and explained that the child was from the Holy Spirit. It is a credit to Joseph's great faith that he then took Mary home as his wife (Matthew 1:18-24).

The groom was to use this time to prepare a dwelling place for his bride, and any children that hopefully would follow. In biblical times, cities were very crowded, so the new home was often created by simply adding another room to his father's house. Thus, when the groom left the bride after the betrothal ceremony, a parting comment might be, "I am going to prepare a place for you."

The Wedding Celebration

The Hebrew word for the wedding celebration translates as "carried away." This was a graphic description, as the bride would be waiting for the groom to carry her away to their new home. The day for this ceremony was decided by the father of the groom, who first had to approve of the newly constructed dwelling. No one other than the father of the groom knew when that day would be. So if the groom were asked when the wedding was going to take place, he would truthfully answer, "Only my father knows."

Since the exact day of the wedding was unsure, the bride and her bridal party would gather at her home every evening towards the end of the year of betrothal. Her bridal party would consist of other unmarried young women. Jerusalem in the time of Jesus was very crowded. Houses were small and often built on top of other houses. Each house had some sort of patio area, and in the evenings social life would be outdoors on these patios where it was cool and pleasant. There also the bridal parties would be anxiously gathered, wondering if that night would be the night the groom would come to carry off his bride. This could go on for weeks. Even in the late evening, the bridal party would keep their oil lamps ready just in case the groom surprised them at that late hour.

When the father of the groom finally said the time had arrived, one of the groom's party would run ahead to the house of the bride and call out, "Behold, the bridegroom comes." This would be followed by the sound of the ram's horn trumpet (shofar), used to proclaim holy days and special events. This would give the bride just a few moments notice that the groom was leading his procession through the streets to claim her. Once he arrived, the bridal party would join the groom's party. Each member of the bridal party would carry a lamp for the lighted procession back to his father's house.

There, the wedding canopy was already set up, and under it a cup of wine was blessed and shared by the couple. Final vows were exchanged. Then the bride and groom would at last retire to their newly constructed room and consummate the marriage. The groom's best friend would stand near the door and listen for the groom's voice. The groom would tell him when the marriage was official, and the friend would announce it to the crowd of guests. The following celebration would last seven days, and on the last day would be a great marriage supper honoring the newlyweds.

Christian Symbolism

Now we will take a biblical walk through these fascinating customs, keeping an eye out for Christian symbolism.

1. **The father of the groom selected a bride for his son.**

    John 6:44: "Jesus answered, 'No one can come to me unless the Father who sent me draws him.'"

    John 17:24: "Father, I want those you have given me to be with me where I am."

    God selects those who will become the bride of His Son, Christ. This is too important to be relegated to a matchmaker.

2. **The contract proposed by the groom told what support and care he would be providing for his bride.**

    John 5:24: "I tell you the truth, whoever hears my word and believes him who sent me has eternal life and will not be condemned."

John 4:14: "Whoever drinks the water I give him will never thirst. Indeed, water I give him will become in him a spring of water welling up to eternal life."

In the case of Jesus, the contract includes eternal life, freedom from condemnation for sin, and the Holy Spirit.

3. And what does the bride bring to the marriage?

John 15:9-12: "As the Father has loved me, so have I loved you. Now remain in my love. If you obey my commands, you will remain in my love, just as I have obeyed my Father's commands and remain in his love. I have told you this so that my joy may be in you and that your joy may be complete. My command is this: Love each other as I have loved you."

Jesus seeks our obedience to His commands and the commands of His Father, and that we love one another as He loved us. In doing this, we receive joy.

4. A valuable dowry is offered by the father of the groom.

John 3:16: "For God so loved the world that he gave his one and only Son, that whoever believes in him shall not perish but have eternal life."

This is the only time in history that the dowry consisted of the life of the groom.

5. **The bride always has the right to refuse the contract:**

Matthew 10:32: "Whoever acknowledges me before men,
I will also acknowledge Him before my Father in heaven.
But whoever disowns me before men, I will also disown
him before my Father in heaven."

Anyone has the right to accept or reject Jesus as their Savior.

6. **The contract, if accepted, meant the bride had been bought**
with a price, and belonged to her husband:

1 Corinthians 6:20: "You are not your own; you were
bought at a price. Therefore honor God with your body."

As the bride of Christ, members of the Church belong to Him
and are to keep themselves pure.

We now move to the acceptance of the contractual agreement
and the betrothal ceremony. This includes the ritual cleansing bath
and the cup of wine, which was blessed and shared by bride and
groom. The proposal of Jesus to His Church bride took place at
His Last Supper, which was a Passover feast. A great deal of symbolism related to Passover occurs here. His proposal to the disciples on that night is carried forth as His proposal to us today.

7. The ritual cleansing bath, to purify the bride before the engagement ceremony.

John 13:1-5 [abbreviated]: *"Having loved his own who were in the world, he now showed them the full extent of his love. He got up, took off his outer clothing, and wrapped a towel around his waist. After that, he poured water into a basin and began to wash his disciples' feet."*

This bathing of feet in the time of Jesus would normally be done by a slave. By this act, Jesus showed the disciples how He would serve His bride, and how we are to serve one another: selflessly, humbly and devotedly. In Christianity today, the ritual cleansing bath can be seen in the rite of baptism.

Matthew 28:19: "Therefore go and make disciples of all nations, baptizing them in the name of the Father and of the Son and of the Holy Spirit, and teaching them to obey everything I have commanded you."

Interestingly, we can also engage in baptism by the study of God's Word:

Ephesians 5:26: "Husbands, love your wives, just as Christ loved the church and gave himself up for her to make her holy, cleansing her by the washing with water through the word, and to present her to himself as a radiant church."

Thus, we see that the study of God's Word in Scripture is in itself like baptism.

8. The contract (covenant) summarized, the wine cup is shared.

Matthew 26:27-29: "Then he took the cup, gave thanks and offered it to them saying, 'Drink from it, all of you. This is my blood of the covenant, which is poured out for many for the forgiveness of sins.'"

In sealing the contract with this cup of wine, Jesus is introducing a New Covenant, which is sanctified by His blood.

On the night before Jesus knew He would be crucified, He proposed to His bride, the disciples, and through them the future Church. All accepted except Judas, who left the dinner to betray Him (the bride can refuse the contract). This began the period of betrothal. Again, by Jewish custom the couple at betrothal was considered married, and only the groom had the right to end the marriage by religious divorce from this point forward. Fortunately, Jesus promised He would never use this option: "And surely I am with you always, to the very end of the age" (Matthew 28:20).

In Christianity, this is the period in which we find ourselves today. We are the Bride of Christ, and anxiously await His return, faithful to Him and the promise that He will return for us.

9. **The betrothal period was a time for the bride to develop purity and modesty.**

   2 Corinthians 11:1-2: "I promised you to one husband, Christ, so that I might present you as a pure virgin to him."

   The Christian's duty is to remain pure so as not to embarrass ourselves or our groom on that day when He comes to claim us as His bride.

10. **The betrothal period was a time for the groom to prepare their future dwelling place.**

    John 14:1-4: "In my Father's house are many rooms; if it were not so, I would have told you. I am going there to prepare a place for you. And if I go and prepare a place for you, I will come back and take you to be with me that you also may be where I am."

11. **Only the groom's father knew when the betrothal period would end and the groom will come to claim his bride.**

    In Matthew 24 we find the disciples asking Jesus when He would return and when the end of the age would come. He answers:

    Matthew 24:36: "No one knows about that day or hour, not even the angels in heaven, nor the Son, but only the Father."

12. Toward the end of the betrothal period, which by Jewish custom would last about a year, the bride would gather her bridal party around her every night, anticipating the coming of the groom. This could go on for weeks. Jesus used this custom to speak of His return in a parable in Matthew 25:1-13, The Parable of the Ten Virgins.

In this parable we find ten virgin bridesmaids who take their lamps and go out to meet the bridegroom. As we have reviewed, they would be taking these lamps onto the patio of the bride's house where they would await the coming of the groom. We are told that five of the virgins were foolish and five were wise. The word "foolish" in the Bible is used as a significant insult, referring to those who either do not know the will and laws of God, or do know but are voluntarily disobedient. The word "wise" means just the opposite, and is a very great compliment.

We are then told that although the foolish virgins took their lamps with them, they took no oil. The wise took oil in jars along with their lamps. Here it must be explained that oil in the Bible is consistently used to symbolize the Holy Spirit of God. Thus, we have five wise virgins who carry the Holy Spirit, the source of their illumination, with them. The five foolish ones do not.

The bridegroom is a long time in coming, and the entire bridal party falls asleep. At midnight the call comes from the approaching procession of the bridegroom. All awaken, and the foolish ones ask the wise for some of their oil. The wise answer that if they give some of their oil away, there might not be enough for both, and advise the foolish to go and find someone who will sell them the oil.

While the foolish are on their way to buy oil, the bridegroom comes and takes the virgins who were ready to the wedding banquet. Then it says, "And the door was shut." Later the others came and asked admittance. Significantly, it does not say that they now had oil. The groom tells the foolish virgins that he does not know them, and they are not allowed in.

Jesus uses this wedding parable to explain that the kingdom of heaven is exclusive to those who have the Holy Spirit and are thereby prepared when He comes to claim His bride at His Second Coming.

13. **In the Jewish wedding tradition, someone from the groom's party would run ahead to announce the approach of his procession with a shout and a trumpet blast.** Then the groom would arrive to carry his bride back to their new home, the wedding feast, and their new life together:
Matthew 24:31: "And He will send his angels with a loud trumpet call, and they will gather the elect from the four winds, from one end of the heavens to the other."
1 Thessalonians 4:16-18: "For the Lord himself will come down from heaven, with a loud command, with the voice of the archangel and with the trumpet call of God, and the

dead in Christ will rise first. After that, we who are still alive and are left will be caught up together with them in the clouds to meet the Lord in the air. And so we will be with the Lord forever."

No one less than an archangel will announce the return of Christ, and the trumpet blast will be the call of God.

14. After the bride is carried back to the groom's house, another cup of wine is shared by the bride and groom. At the Last Supper, Jesus told us He would wait until He came to get us before drinking this cup or any other wine:

Matthew 26:29: "I tell you, I will not drink of this fruit of the vine from now on until that day when I drink it anew with you in my Father's kingdom."

Jesus was revealing how much He cares for us in saying this. He was saying that He would not drink wine again until He can share it with us.

In the church today, we seldom speak of consummation with Christ; yet this is one of our greatest promises in the Bible. Our wedding is consummated as we are given glorified bodies and unite in Christ:

Ephesians 5:31: "For this reason a man will leave his father and mother and be united to his wife, and the two will become one flesh. This is a profound mystery - but I am talking about Christ and the church."

Philippians 3:20-21: "But our citizenship is in heaven. And we eagerly await a Savior from there, the Lord Jesus Christ, who, by the power that enables him to bring everything under his control, will transform our lowly bodies so that they will be like his glorious body."

1 Corinthians 15:51-52, 42-44: "Listen, I tell you a mystery: We will not all sleep, but we will all be changed - in a flash, in the twinkling of an eye, at the last trumpet. For the trumpet will sound, the dead will be raised imperishable, and we will be changed. The body that is sown is perishable, it is raised imperishable; it is sown in dishonor, it is raised in glory; it is sown in weakness, it is raised in power; it is sown a natural body, it is raised a spiritual body."

Our new bodies will be imperishable, glorious, powerful and spiritual.

15. And finally, the wedding celebration.

Revelation 19:6-8:

"Hallelujah!

For our Lord God Almighty reigns.

Let us rejoice and be glad and give him glory!

For the wedding of the Lamb has come,

And the bride has made herself ready.

Fine linen, bright and clean, was given her to wear.

(Fine linen stands for the righteous acts of the saints.)"

At the wedding, we are given a linen garment that represents our righteousness.

Note the word "given," for our righteousness is by grace, and not earned by acts.

The passage continues, "Then the angel said to me, 'Write: Blessed are those who are invited to the wedding supper of the Lamb!'"

CHAPTER 14 QUESTIONS FOR DISCUSSION

1. How should Christians respond to the knowledge that God specifically chose them to be the bride of Christ? (John 6:44, 17:24)

2. What does Jesus offer to His bride, the church? (John 4:14, 5:24)

3. What can we offer Christ as our wedding gift to Him? (John 15:9-12, 2 Corinthians 11:1-2)

4. Read again the parable of the wise and foolish virgins (Matthew 25: 1-13). Biblically speaking, would you say you are foolish or wise? What part of this parable has the greatest impact on you?

5. We will receive spiritual bodies when Christ returns for us (Philippians 3: 20-21, 1 Corinthians 15: 42-44, 51-52). Until that time, what attitude should you have toward the body God gave you? What action could you take to be consistent with that attitude?

APPENDIX 1

Judaism 101:
An Overview of Jewish History

To understand the religion of Jesus, it is helpful to know the history of the Jews. The following is a much-abbreviated history of a people who have existed for thousands of years.

Jewish history begins with Abraham, about 2150 B.C. Abraham was the son of an idol maker. He is credited with introducing monotheism, which means there is only one God. Monotheism is an essential tenet of Judaism; to this day, the watchword of the Jewish faith is, "Hear O Israel, the Lord our God, the Lord is One!"

There are two ancient legends about Abraham that bear telling. In the first, we find him minding his father's idol store. A man comes in and admires a certain idol. He asks Abraham if the idol will bring him a good harvest.

Abraham asks, "How old are you?"

"I am a man of forty years," is the reply.

Abraham then states, "You are a man of forty years, and yet that idol was made last week. Only a fool would believe it could affect his crops!"

In the second legend, we again find Abraham minding the store. When his father returns, he finds that all the idols in the store have been broken into pieces except one large idol in the corner. Next to this idol is a large stick. In shock, he asks his son what happened.

Abraham replies, "The most amazing thing! While you were gone, that idol came to life, picked up that stick, and shattered all the others!"

His astonished father cries, "Idols can't do that!"

Abraham answers, "You are right, Father, idols can do nothing."

Because of Abraham's faith, God established a Covenant with him. This Covenant has three parts (detailed in Genesis 12:1-3, 13:14-16, and 15:9-18):

- **Land:** A distinct homeland for the Jewish people. The area described consists of modern day Israel, with significantly expanded borders that would include Lebanon, Syria, Iraq and Egypt.
- **Seed:** That Abraham would be the father of a great people.

- **Blessing:** God would bless Abraham and his descendants, and all the earth would be blessed by them.

The importance of the Covenant cannot be overstated. It is the beginning of the Jews as God's chosen people.

There are three patriarchs of Judaism: Abraham is the first. His son Isaac follows. Abraham had another son before Isaac, named Ishmael, conceived with his wife's servant. Ishmael becomes the father of the Arab peoples. Isaac's son, Jacob, is the third patriarch. He was later renamed Israel. Jacob had a son named Joseph who had quite an eventful life. He ended up highly favored in Egypt, and moved his family there, including Jacob.

The Jewish population in Egypt grew so large that Pharaoh became apprehensive. He decided to control them by enslaving them, and they remained slaves in Egypt for 400 years. God heard their prayers of suffering and planned deliverance for them led by Moses, about 1500 B.C. God Himself rescued the Jews from Egypt using a series of plagues to pressure Pharaoh into releasing them. These plagues were ushered in by God's servant, Moses. After the tenth plague, Pharaoh allowed the Jews to leave. The Egyptians were moved by God to give them parting gifts of much gold, silver, and fine linen.

Moses continued to lead the Jews for 40 years through the desert, being fed by manna, which fell from heaven daily. They were being prepared to enter and conquer the Promised Land of the Covenant. During this time, Moses taught them God's laws and received the Ten Commandments. Jewish feasts and holy days were established, (enumerated in Exodus) and the priesthood was established. A system of sacrifices to make atonement with God was reestablished. The Tabernacle was constructed, using the gold, silver, and fine linen from Egypt. The Tabernacle was the all-important dwelling place of God among His chosen people, as well as the place where the tablets of God's laws were kept. The Tabernacle became the model for the future Temple.

After the Jews conquered the Promised Land with God aiding their military campaigns, a period of anarchy ensued. Idolatry resumed as the Jews took on the customs of their pagan neighbors. They desired a king in accordance with the peoples around them. This began the age of prophets and kings, and God then spoke to His people through prophets. The first prophet of God was Samuel. He anointed the first king, Saul. Saul was not a good king and had episodes of faithlessness, cruelty, and paranoid behavior. After he died in battle with the Philistines, he was succeeded by King David in about 1000 B.C.

David was the great warrior-king of Israel and led Israel to greatness, establishing Jerusalem as the capital city and acquiring great wealth for the nation. He had a son, Solomon, whose reign began about 950 B.C.

Solomon built the first Temple in Jerusalem on Mt. Moriah (where Abraham was asked by God to sacrifice Isaac as a sign of his faith; also the site of today's Islamic Dome of the Rock). All sacrifices for atonement occurred at the Temple. The high court of the Jews, the Sanhedrin, met there as well. The seven yearly festivals were also celebrated at the Temple. Three of them, Passover, Pentecost, and Tabernacles, mandated attendance by all Jews, who were required to make a pilgrimage to Jerusalem three times a year for this purpose.

After the kingship of Solomon, the Hebrews split into the Southern kingdom of Judea and the Northern kingdom of Israel. Judea retained the holy city of Jerusalem as its capital. Both kingdoms strayed from God's commandments and both indulged in idolatry. Judea, however, periodically had a righteous king who ushered in repentance and returned to worshipping the One True God. The Northern kingdom of Israel, however, was consistent in idol worship and refused to do God's will.

In 721 B.C., the Northern kingdom of Israel was overrun by Assyria. The ten tribes that made up that kingdom were taken into exile and lost to history; however, a remnant of each of the tribes was preserved in Judea, having moved there to continue to worship the true God at His Temple.

Alas, in 586 B.C. the Southern kingdom of Judea was overrun by the Babylonians. The great Temple of Solomon was completely destroyed. The Jews were led into exile; miraculously, they were released 70 years later. Returning to Judea, they rebuilt the Temple in 515 B.C. The Temple remained in this rebuilt form for the most part until 20 B.C., when Herod began to expand and rebuild it into one of the great wonders of the world — this was the Temple of the time of Jesus.

The Romans occupied all of the lands of the Jews in 63 B.C. Temple sacrifices and ceremonies were allowed to continue, but exploitation of the Jews and the Temple wealth led to periodic rebellion. Many of the Jewish leaders of this time were corrupt and worked closely with the Romans. Great divisions developed among the Jews as to how to live under the Romans. Many of the Jews believed that God would send the long-awaited Messiah, who, according to ancient prophetic Scripture, would liberate the Jews and restore Israel to independent greatness. Many false messiahs and revolutionaries (zealots) came forth. On several occasions, these false messiahs raised armies and attacked the Romans, but always with disastrous results.

Jesus began His three-year ministry about 30 A.D. Claiming to be the true Messiah and the one true Son of God, He performed healings and miracles, drawing a significant following. A large part of His teachings challenged the Jewish leadership at that time and their ritualistic practices. He preached strongly for social reform. Although His message never encouraged violence, some of the Jewish leaders became concerned that the masses following after Jesus might alarm the Romans and result in military reprisal. Other leaders were frightened of losing their power over the people because His teachings frequently challenged their religious behaviors. In the end, a small group of Jewish leaders turned Him over to the Romans. Jesus offered no defense at His own trial, and although there was no evidence that He had broken Roman law, a Roman leader had Him flogged and crucified.

This crucifixion of Jesus occurred on the holiday of Passover. Three days after the crucifixion, on the holiday of First Fruits, His tomb was found empty and He was seen risen in physical form by some of His followers. Many more sightings occurred over the next several weeks. Still other followers experienced being filled with the Holy Spirit seven weeks after the Resurrection, on the holiday of Pentecost. The Church was born, made up entirely of Jews who believed Jesus was the long-awaited Messiah.

Throughout the time of Jesus, the land of Israel was under Roman rule. Much of the Jewish leadership was corrupt, and life was very difficult for the Jewish people. About 40 years after the crucifixion, in 70 A.D., Roman oppression and exploitation of the Jews reached an intolerable level. This led to the First Jewish Revolt. It was disastrous for the Jews. During fighting in Jerusalem, 500,000 Jews were killed and the Temple of Herod was set afire. When Herod built the Temple, he had it crowned richly in gold. As the gold melted from the fire, it seeped between the massive stones of the Temple walls. Later, the Romans tore down the charred remains of the Temple stone by stone to retrieve the gold.

Roman oppression continued. In 130 A.D., the Second Jewish Revolt erupted. This is also called the Bar Kochba Rebellion. It was named for its leader, Bar Kochba, who was a military genius and leader of a band of rebels. The most prominent rabbi of Israel at that time, Rabbi Akiba, declared Bar Kochba to be the true Messiah. Almost all of Judea believed he was the one they had been waiting for, and there was unified rebellion. Initially the Jews achieved great success and the Romans were driven out of Judea. An independent Jewish state was established, which lasted for three years. The Romans then returned, determined to put a final end to the Jewish revolts. In the earlier uprising of 70 A.D. the Romans attacked with three legions — this time they brought 13, and this time one million Jews were killed in the fighting. Leadership of the priesthood was fully discredited. The Romans built a pagan temple on the site of the Jewish Temple, and declared that Israel could no longer exist as a nation. They renamed the land Palestine, insulting the Jews by naming it after their ancient enemy, the Philistines. The surviving Jews were ultimately dispersed throughout the world, and this dispersion is known as the *Diaspora*.

In these destructive years, three key parts of ancient Judaism were lost: the Temple with the sacrifices, the priesthood, and the Jewish theocracy. Without the Temple, religious life as practiced by the Jews for centuries had come to an end. The need to redefine Judaism was necessary if they were to survive as a unique people.

A key problem was finding a way to achieve atonement without the temple sacrifices. This situation was not without precedent, however. After the destruction of Solomon's Temple in 586 B.C., the Jews could not offer sacrifices for 70 years; during this time of exile in Babylonia, the prophet Daniel maintained righteousness by praying fervently and following God's laws.

Based on the precedent of Daniel, the Jewish leadership decided that prayer, study of God's Word, charitable works and ethical behavior would take the place of sacrifices in bringing the people to righteousness before God. Rabbis, well educated in the law and Jewish customs, would function as the spiritual leaders and teachers for local Jewish communities. The local synagogue would replace the Temple as a gathering place for the people and would serve as a house of worship. These modifications to the previous religious practices at the Temple have become known as Rabbinic Judaism, and continue to this day.

Although much of significance happens to the Jews over the next 2,000 years (see appendix on Christian anti-Semitism), the two most important events are the Holocaust and the formation of the State of Israel.

In the Holocaust, six million Jews were systematically exterminated by the Nazis, and are still recovering spiritually and emotionally from this unimaginable horror.

And in 1948, for the first time in 2,000 years, the Jews again had an independent state in their promised homeland of Israel. In the 1960s, in response to being attacked by the Arabs, the Jews again gained control of Jerusalem, the ancient capital city of David.

Today, there are about 14 million Jews in the world according to a 1990s census, and the population is roughly divided throughout the world as follows:

- Israel: 5 million
- United States: 6 million
- Russia and the Ukraine: 1 million
- France: 600,000 (less than 1 million in western Europe)

APPENDIX 2

Questions Christians Commonly Ask About Jews

What do Jews believe about the afterlife?

There is not a unified Jewish view of death and afterlife. There is a general rabbinical consensus that an afterlife occurs, but the specific details about it are considered unknowable. Heaven is embraced as an idea, but it is not described. Of the various explanations considered in Judaism for the afterlife, there are two major possibilities:

- Immortality, the continued existence of the soul after life has left the body.

- Resurrection, the eventual return of the soul to its original physical body after physical death.

Both positions have had adherents over the centuries. Many modern Jews believe in the immortality of the soul, recognizing that the human spirit has a divine nature, and like the divine it will exist forever. Others hold to the idea of an eventual bodily resurrection in the final days, with the soul then reuniting with the resurrected physical body.

What Jews consider knowable is that death is in God's hands, and each person departs this life at God's appointed time. God is always just in death, however untimely or unfair the demise of an individual may appear.

What happened to the animal sacrifices?

Soon after leaving Egypt, God gave meticulous instructions for sacrifices to be performed by the priesthood of the Jews. These could only be performed in the outer courtyard of the Tabernacle, and later in the Temple at Jerusalem. One of the purposes of the sacrifices was to achieve atonement for sin, and this required shedding of blood: "For the life of a creature is in the blood, and I have given it to you to make atonement for yourselves on the altar; it is the blood that makes atonement for one's life" (Leviticus 17:11).

At the time of Jesus, the land of Israel was under Roman rule. Much of the Jewish leadership was corrupt, and life was very difficult for the Jewish people. About 40 years after the Crucifixion, in 70 A.D., Roman oppression and exploitation of the Jews reached an intolerable level. This led to the First Jewish Revolt. It was disastrous for the Jews, as 500,000 were killed and the Temple was torn down by the Romans.

Without the Temple, religious life as practiced by the Jews for centuries had come to an end. A key problem was finding a way to achieve atonement without the Temple sacrifices. Yet, this situation was not without precedent. After the destruction of Solomon's Temple in 586 B.C., the Jews could not offer sacrifices for 70 years until the Temple was rebuilt. During this time of exile in Babylonia, the prophet Daniel maintained righteousness and favor with God without the Temple. He did this by praying fervently, following God's laws, doing what he could to help the community in which he found himself, and behaving ethically.

Based on this precedent, it was decided that prayer, study of God's Word, charitable works and ethical behavior would take the place of sacrifices in bringing the people to righteousness before God. Rabbis, well educated in the law and Jewish customs, would function as the spiritual leaders and teachers for local Jewish communities. The local synagogue would replace the Temple as a gathering place for the people and would serve as a house of worship. These modifications to the previous religious practices at the Temple have become known as Rabbinic Judaism, and continue to this day.

What do the Jews think about Hebrew Bible prophecies concerning Jesus?

That Jesus is clearly and specifically prophesied in the Hebrew Scriptures is challenged by the Jews. Christians often find this surprising, as they seem to find such references plentiful. The difference becomes more understandable when the Jewish viewpoint is respectfully considered.

From the Jewish viewpoint, Jesus is not believed to be the Messiah. They do not approach the reading of the Hebrew Bible with a foreknowledge of the life of Jesus. Rather, Jews enter the study of Scripture looking forward, and so they see prophecies of one who is yet to come. Supporting this view, it must be admitted that in reading the Hebrew Bible from beginning to end, one would not conclude that the Messiah would minister for only three years, that no peace or greatness for Israel would come during His ministry, and that the Messiah would then be crucified. Rather, it reads that the Messiah would usher in an era of greatness and peace for the Jews, with Israel being foremost among all the nations. (Christians explain this seeming incongruity through the promised return of Christ in the future, and His fulfillment of all remaining prophecies at that time as mentioned in Luke 21:25-27 and Revelation 19:11-16.)

In most of the controversies about scriptural prophecy, the question is not whether the text is indeed messianic, but rather if it is specifically referring to Jesus. Arguments about how a given passage should be most accurately translated are frequent. With some justification, there are accusations of taking license with translations to reinforce the point one is trying to make.

We will now consider a few examples of controversial Hebrew Bible passages to shed further light on some Jewish explanations of messianic prophecies.

Psalm 2 contains strong references to an exalted royal son of David, and is messianic in content. In the NIV version, verse 12 reads, "Kiss the Son, lest he be angry," which certainly appears to be a reference to Christ. Yet, a Jewish translation of the same passage would be, "Worship in purity, lest he be angry." This is sometimes cited as an example of Christian bias in translation.

A similar wording controversy is found in Psalm 22. This psalm is one of the most famous of the messianic prophecies pointing to Christ, and begins with His last words on the cross, "My God, My God, why have you forsaken me?" In verse 16, the NIV version reads, "They have pierced my hands and feet." In the Jewish scripture it is translated, "Like a lion they are at my hands and feet." Jews again feel that the Christian translation seems biased towards the Crucifixion.

A much more controversial translation is found in Isaiah 7:14. Here, we read, "A virgin shall conceive..." In Matthew 1:23, this phrase is quoted by Matthew as prophesying the Virgin Mary giving birth to Jesus. Scholastic analysis reveals that the Hebrew word translated as "virgin" in this passage can be better translated as simply a young woman of an age to bear children, whether or not she was married. The passage is thus insufficient as a specific foretelling of a virgin birth, and again the translation may reveal a Christian bias. (Christians counter by pointing out that the better translation does not rule out Mary being a virgin, it simply does not affirm it. Further, the passage goes on to mention a son yet to be born who will be called "Immanuel." This was a name used to refer to Jesus, meaning "God with us.")

This particular passage illustrates yet another controversial area in messianic prophecy. Many Christians consider the New Testament to be the inspired Word of God, and therefore the numerous passages of Hebrew Scripture quoted in the New Testament are accepted as being placed by God's direction. Thus, if Matthew says the prophecy refers to a virgin, the statement will be accepted as a matter of faith. Obviously, the Jews would disagree, believing that the New Testament is not the inspired Word of God.

The final controversy we will discuss is in Isaiah 53. This is an often-quoted passage for those seeking to prove Jesus in the Hebrew scripture. It is controversial in that scholastic analysis shows Isaiah to be speaking of a past historical fact. From this the Jews deduce that the one to which the passage referred has already been killed, although who that person might be is unknown. (The Christian response must include that when all the verses referring to the life and mission and ministry of Jesus in this chapter are reviewed, it is difficult to believe that they rather apply to some other unidentified person lost to history. Additionally, as God is capable of experiencing the past, present and future simultaneously, He may have simply chosen to have this prophet speak in past tense about a future event.)

We conclude by recognizing that messianic prophecies are controversial, and may even reveal bias by translators. Jewish scholars see no convincing reason to believe that any of the hundred-plus messianic prophecies refer specifically to Jesus.

Why don't Jews recognize Jesus as the Messiah, and become Christians?

Since the time of Jesus there has consistently been a minority of Jews who recognized Jesus as the Messiah. It is exciting that over the past several decades this number has grown dramatically. However, the vast majority of Jews still do not believe in Jesus as anything more than a prophet or great teacher. There are many reasons why:

- Among other things, the Messiah was to bring peace and prosperity to Israel. At the time of Jesus, this was expected to occur by military means. King David, the great warrior-king of Israel, was the model of this, and it was from his line that Jesus descended. There was certainly no peace for Israel in the time of Jesus, and there is still no peace for Israel today, so Jews wonder how Jesus could be the Messiah.

The Christian response to this argument is simply that Jesus will return, as clearly stated in the New Testament (Luke 21:25-27, Revelation 19:11-16). At that time, all remaining prophecies concerning the Messiah will be fulfilled.

- The concept of the Trinity in Christianity doesn't make sense to the Jews. The watchword of the Jewish faith is, "Hear O Israel, the Lord our God, the Lord is *One*." In listening to Christians, they hear the Lord is actually three: Father, Son and Holy Spirit. To the Jewish mind this sounds like polytheism. How can one God have three parts? How can the man Jesus also be God?

Admittedly, defining the Trinity is difficult at best, and many are the theological arguments on this subject. Christians bristle at the implication that they are polytheistic, however. The New Testament gives ample evidence that the Father, the Son and the Holy Spirit are divine, that the three are distinct, and that God is one. "The Trinity" is the best that our fallible human language can come up with to describe these seemingly somewhat contradictory truths.

- Salvation apart from works also doesn't make sense to the Jews. A key tenet of Judaism is that righteousness is based on good works. In Christianity, they hear that a person who commits horrible atrocities but comes to Christ on his deathbed goes to heaven, while a Jew with exemplary behavior goes to hell simply for not accepting Jesus. Again, this doesn't make sense to the Jews. The Christian recognizes two different questions presented here:

1. Would God receive an appeal for mercy from a horrible person in the last moments of life?
2. Would God deny entrance into heaven for those who reject His Son?

The response to the first question is not difficult. Both Judaism and Christianity recognize God to be forgiving in His nature (Joel 2:13; 2 Chronicles 7:14). Traditional Judaism would agree that a Jew who had behaved unspeakably could still receive forgiveness on the Day of Atonement as long as his repentance was truly sincere. If this is possible on the Day of Atonement, why not in the last moments of life? The question here is really about the sincerity of a last-moment confession. Christians certainly agree that any acceptance of God must be in sincere faith. Jesus made it clear that He would not acknowledge many who claimed to believe in Him in the end times, revealing that sincere faith must underlie a profession of belief (Matthew 7:21). Therefore, Christianity and Judaism agree that God can forgive those who sincerely beg His forgiveness, regardless of past behavior, providing that the request for forgiveness is based on sincere belief.

Responding to the second question is challenging. Christians believe that acceptance for salvation is based upon Christ's completed work on behalf of man. He is the ultimate atoning sacrifice for the sin of mankind, and therefore God's acceptance of anyone who trusts in His plan is based on the acceptable nature of Christ's perfect life, not ours. Because God is perfect and just, nothing less than a perfect sacrifice for sin will satisfy His judgment. Even if we were mostly righteous, that portion of our life that was unrighteous could not be overlooked by a perfectly righteous, holy, and just God. The unrighteous portion would still require atonement. Christ's sacrifice is satisfactory, even for the deathbed confession, if made by grace through faith (1 Peter 3:18; 2 Corinthians 5:17). The New Testament states clearly that the only path to salvation is through the Son of God (John 3:18; John 14:6). In a society that values inclusion of all, this claim of a singular path to salvation is often decried as cruel. Yet God offers this blessed salvation freely for all who believe, regardless of station in life, past behavior, level of intelligence, gender, race, creed, color or any other condition that describes humanity.

According to Paul in the New Testament, God has a plan for the Jews that includes a temporary hardening towards Jesus. Paul's words hearken back to Isaiah 6:10. In Romans 11:25, he says: "Israel has experienced a hardening in part until the full number of Gentiles has come in." Paul goes on to explain that the plan is for the Jews to have their hearts hardened against Christ for a time.

This allows the Gentile population to have a chance to acknowledge Jesus as Lord. Later in the same passage Paul says, "And so all Israel will be saved." Many Evangelical Christians believe this will happen in the end times, but again only through the recognition of Christ as the source of salvation.

- Christians do not consistently behave in ways that distinguish themselves from the rest of the population. This makes it difficult for Jews to see ready evidence of Christ as a godly influence in their lives.

Sadly, it must be admitted that the overall behavior of Christians often does not stand out from the rest of society. Yet there are myriad testimonies of individual believers who have had a remarkable transformation in their lives attributable to accepting Jesus as their Lord. Added to this are those missionaries who gave up comfort and safety to follow the calling of Christ. So while it may be fair to state that Christians as a whole do not behave differently from the non-believers around them, a large number of individual Christians certainly do.

- Many Jews fear that to become a Christian means they will completely lose the identity that is at the core of their very being. The fear is that accepting Jesus means leaving their culture, their customs, and their Jewish identity.

This certainly need not be the case, as I hope this book has illustrated. There are now Messianic Jewish synagogues where Jews who believe Jesus is the Messiah worship in traditional Jewish ways. Many Jews know that if they were to become Christian, their families will be hurt or angry and might even disown them. Family life is very important to the Jewish people, so many are not even willing to consider the Christian message.

- Anti-Semitism, or behavior of Christians and the Church directly against the Jews, has done more to keep the Jews away from Christ than anything else. This behavior through the centuries has been inexcusable, horrible and unrelenting. The following appendix is an overview of this behavior. It is eye-opening to many Christians, and well known to most Jews.

APPENDIX 3

An Overview of Christian Anti-Semitism

Christian Anti-Semitism originated from several non-biblical but widely held Christian beliefs. These beliefs resulted in horrible persecution against the Jews, starting almost at the beginning of the Church, and have continued throughout history, even into our time. Most Christians are unaware of the tremendous amount of persecution perpetrated on the Jews in the name of Christ through the centuries. The Jews, however, tend to be quite aware of these atrocities, and of course this greatly hinders evangelism.

There are two non-biblical but widely held beliefs that have led to most Christian anti-Semitism. The first is that the Jews killed Christ, and therefore deserve to be persecuted, even to this day. The second is that the Church has permanently replaced the Jews as God's favored people.

In believing that the Jews killed Christ, many who claim to follow Christ feel justified in punishing the Jews for slaying Him. Yet, if we simply look at the words of Jesus and then the facts of His trial and the crucifixion, several Biblical and logical flaws in this reasoning become apparent.

Although Jewish leaders did bring charges against Jesus and sought to have Him killed, it is important to realize that the crucifixion was a part of God's plan for our salvation. Jesus knew this, and so willingly went to the Crucifixion in obedience to His Father, as He tells us in John 10:17-18, "The reason my Father loves me is that I lay down my life - only to take it up again. No one takes it from me, but I lay it down of my own accord. I have authority to lay it down and authority to take it up again." It is further evident in Scripture that He could have avoided crucifixion in a number of ways, including defending Himself at His trial (Matthew 27:14), calling on God for an angelic rescue (Matthew 26:53), staying away from Jerusalem (Matthew 16:21), slipping through the crowd (John 10:39), or probably many other means. Yet because He so loves us and God, He chose to submit to the will of His Father (Matthew 26:42).

Additionally, the Jews had no right to crucify criminals under Roman law. It was actually Romans, while recognizing Jesus to be innocent of the charges brought against Him by Jewish leaders, who crucified Him anyway (Luke 23:22). Interestingly, the Church has never persecuted Romans.

Furthermore, the charges brought against Jesus were made by a small handful of Jews. There were only about 5,000-7,000 Pharisees and about 2,000 Sadducees at the time of Jesus, out of a total Jewish population of several million. Therefore blaming and persecuting all Jews for killing Christ seems a bit unjust, as does blaming and persecuting Jews born since that time. After all, how many Christians would be comfortable being judged for the actions of all others who claimed to follow Christ?

Replacement Theology is the belief system that the Church has become the new favored people of God, while all Jews have permanently lost favor with Him and He doesn't ever want them back. This doctrine began in the First Century Church and opened the gates to future anti-Semitism. By this thinking, Christian acts against the Jews are actually favored by God, or at least such acts don't upset a God who disdains the Jews anyway.

Yet to accept this view, Christians must ignore our own accepted Scripture, especially Romans 11. Here Paul states quite clearly that there has always been a Jewish remnant that retained favor with God. However, many Jews transgressed against God. Salvation came to the Gentiles in part to make Israel envious. By becoming envious, the Jews would hopefully be led to Christ. Paul is careful to point out that the Gentiles came into God's kingdom by being grafted into the olive tree (of Israel). They were not to think of themselves as an entirely new tree. Gentiles receive nourishment from the sap of the original olive root, but were not to boast or take pride in being those new branches. The root of Israel supports them — they do not support the root.

Paul goes on to say: "Consider therefore the kindness and sternness of God: sternness to those who fell, but kindness to you, provided that you continue in his kindness. Otherwise, you also will be cut off. And if they [the Jews who were broken off] do not persist in unbelief, they will be grafted in again, for God is able to graft them in again" (Romans 11:22).

Putting Paul's thoughts together:

- God always maintains a favored remnant of the Jews as part of His plan.

- As some Jews transgressed against God, salvation came to the Gentiles in part to make the Jews envious.

- The envy was to be evoked because the Gentiles were to exhibit a godly kindness to one another and to Jews. By that envy, the Jews who were cut off might not persist in unbelief, but rather be grafted back into the tree. Gentiles who abandon God's kindness and grace are threatened with being cut off.

- Christians should act as Jesus instructed in John 15:12, "My command is this: Love each other as I have loved you." If they did, then Jews might envy what they demonstrate and come to Christ.

This is God's plan for Christian behavior and the hoped-for Jewish response, according to Paul. Can we, the Church, take pride in having accomplished this?

A Review of Christian Anti-Semitic History

Early Christian Writings: By the early second century, the split between Christianity and Judaism was growing. On the Christian side, there was a moving away from Jewish tradition and ceremony as the Church tried to define itself. Many of the early Church fathers wrote against Judaism and Jews in general, according to the beliefs of Replacement Theology, and that the Jews were all to be blamed for the death of Christ. Some of these writings encouraged violence. This culminated in the Council of Nicea in 325 A.D. As Constantine unified the Roman Empire by converting it to Christianity, a number of compromises were made with the pagan population that separated the Church from its Jewish roots. The Jewish calendar was replaced with the pagan calendar. Celebration of the Resurrection was moved from First Fruits of the Jewish calendar to Easter, the spring festival when the pagans worshipped Ishtar. The Crucifixion was separated from Passover and rescheduled on Good Friday. The Sabbath was moved to Sunday, the day set aside to worship the sun god. In 440 A.D., the Church arbitrarily assigned December 25 as the date of the birth of Jesus to accommodate the pagans, who believed this to be the day of the birth of the sun.

The Birth of Rabbinic Judaism: On the Jewish side, there was much upheaval during these years. With the Temple destroyed, 1.5 million Jews killed by the Romans and the loss of the ancient system of worship and sacrifices, Judaism desperately set about to redefine itself so it could survive as the Jewish population was being dispersed throughout the world. Out of this chaos, Rabbinic Judaism was born. The rabbi would be the spiritual leader of his community. Atonement would no longer come from blood sacrifices, but rather from prayer, the study of God's Word, charitable works and ethical behavior. The synagogue would take the place of the Temple as a gathering place and a place to study God's Word. Ultimately, it was also decided that those who were truly Jewish could not believe that Jesus was God.

The anti-Jewish sentiments of the developing Church grew over time. Writings and preaching against the Jews grew into social restrictions, legal restrictions and physical violence. The following history of Christian anti-Semitism is well known by the Jews. It is important for Christians to be familiar with it as well, that they might understand the suspicion, distrust, and even anger Jews often feel when approached with Christianity.

Spanish Council of Elvira (306): The council prohibited marriage and all social interaction between Jews and Christians. Landholders were forbidden to sell produce to Jews, so as to prevent the Jews from saying a blessing over the produce.

Justinian Code (534): Jews and other non-Christians lose their Roman citizenship.

Synod of Carthage (535): Jews were forbidden to be judges and tax collectors, and prohibited from owning slaves. This last restriction prevented them from owning agricultural land.

Persecution in Spain (613): Jews were given the choice of leaving Spain or converting to Christianity. Most were robbed of their wealth. Jewish children over six years of age were taken from their parents and given a Christian upbringing.

The Crusades (11ᵗʰ, 12ᵗʰ and 13ᵗʰ Centuries): The Crusades were military expeditions conducted under the authority and with the blessing of the Church. The purpose was to recover the Holy Land from the Moslems and stop the spread of Islam. Many Crusaders felt this was an opportunity to rid the world of all infidels and slaughtered thousands of Jews as well. Much of this killing took place in Europe, with 12,000 Jews murdered in the Rhine Valley alone. In France, 140 Jewish communities were destroyed and 5,000 Jews were burned at the stake. When the Crusaders arrived in Jerusalem, the local Jews were herded into the synagogue, which was set on fire, and the Jews burned alive while the Crusaders sang, "Christ, We Adore Thee."

The Plague Years (1347-1350): The great plagues of Europe claimed about one-third to one-fourth of the total European population. Plague was carried by rat fleas. The Jews followed the laws of Moses and kept fastidious households, so Jewish villages had few rats and little death from plague. Christian homes were not kept as clean, so Christian villages had a much higher plague rate. Noticing this, the Christians decided that the Jews must be causing the plague by poisoning their wells, and in retaliation wiped out entire villages of Jews.

The Spanish and Portuguese Inquisitions (15th and 16th Centuries): Church leaders tortured and murdered tens of thousands of true Christians who were falsely accused of being heretics. In addition, they murdered hundreds of thousands of Jews, believing the Jews would be better off if they cried out to Christ while being burned alive at the stake than if they were left alone. Many Jews were given the choice of accepting baptism or exile. If they accepted baptism, they had to renounce their religion. If they refused to be baptized, their property was confiscated and sold to the highest bidder. Many were forced to leave the country with nothing.

Martin Luther's Writings (1542-1543): Two pamphlets written by Luther in these years contain some of the most malicious language ever used against the Jews. He proposed that synagogues and Jewish schools be burned and that Jews be transferred to isolated community settlements (ghettos). He wanted to confiscate all Jewish literature and prohibit rabbis from teaching under penalty of death. He urged that their wealth be taken from them and used to support new converts to Christianity. He taught that Jews should be forced to do manual labor as a form of penance. (Hitler was to use the writings of Luther in later years.) Luther's final comment on the Jews was, "We are at fault for not slaying them." (Some leaders in the Evangelical Lutheran Church in America have agreed finally to issue a statement repudiating Luther's words and apologize to the Jews for their past anti-Semitism).

The Cossack Massacres (1648-1649): During the peasant revolt against Polish rule in the Ukraine, over 100,000 Jews were killed and 300 communities destroyed.

The Russian Pogroms (1881-1921): Fleeing western European persecution, millions of Jews settled in Poland. Russia conquered many bordering states, including Poland, and found herself with an unwanted population of millions of Jews. The solution for this "Jewish problem" was the Pogrom, which translates as "destruction." One-third was deported, one-third faced forced conversion, and one-third was starved to death. Looting, rape, and murder of the Jews were common. Those who fled to the west entered the Holocaust.

Protocols of the Elders of Aion (1900): This is a hate-filled and hate-inducing book which claims to expose a Jewish conspiracy to rule the world by controlling banking, arms, political power and culture. It is complete fabrication, actually having been written by the Russian secret police to discredit the Bolshevik enemies of Czar Nicholas II, many of who were Jewish. This book was used by Hitler as support for his attacks on the Jews, by Stalin to root Jews out of respected positions in the Communist party, and has been widely circulated throughout the Arab world since the establishment of Israel. It was widely circulated at the United Nations Conference on Racism in 2002.

French Jewish Deportation (1940s): The Vichy government of France collaborated with Nazi Germany, deporting 75,000 Jews to Nazi death camps. Only 2,500 survived.

The Holocaust (1939-1944): In *Mein Kampf* Hitler wrote, "Hence today I believe that I am acting in accordance with the

Almighty Creator; by defending myself against the Jew, I am fighting for the work of the Lord." Hitler's followers, acting under the sign of the broken cross (swastika), systematically killed six million Jews in death camps. At their height, some of the camps could kill 25,000 people a day. This reduced the Jewish population of Europe from nine million in 1939 to about three million by the end of the war. Although the Nazis were not Christian, they did represent Christian Europe to the Jewish mind, and it is fair to ask, "Where were the Christians during the Holocaust?" Out of 14,000 German evangelical pastors in 1933, only 800 refused to sign the Nazi oath.

The United Nations Conference on Racism (2002): Boycotted by the United States and mostly ignored by the American press, this conference became a frenzy of anti-Semitism, with anti-Jewish literature being distributed and Zionism (the movement for having a Jewish homeland in Israel) being equated to Nazism. The Conference on Racism became a Conference of Racists. Though the hatred came primarily from the Arabs, there was no significant opposition.

Is it any surprise that the Jews feel uneasy in our world and are reluctant to trust Christians, much less come to Christ?

In Matthew 28:19 Jesus gives His parting words to His disciples: "All authority in heaven and earth has been given to me.

Therefore go and make disciples of *all nations*, baptizing in the name of the Father and of the Son and of the Holy Spirit, and teaching them to obey everything I have commanded you. And surely I am with you always, to the very end of the age."

"All nations" certainly includes the Jews. There is a tremendous amount of work yet to be done by the followers of Jesus, and the work is all the more difficult because of previous behavior of those claiming to act in His name. Yet in encouragement, Jesus begins this last instruction to us by revealing that all authority in heaven and earth has been given to Him, and ends with His assurance that He will be with us always.

For those who are cruel and abusive to the Jews, Scripture does not portend well. There is no scriptural reason to believe that there has been an end to God's promise to Abraham (Genesis 12:3), "I will bless those who bless you, and whoever curses you I will curse." Additionally, the prophets on numerous occasions announced God's eventual cataclysmic wrath on the enemies of His chosen people (Joel 3; Obadiah 15-18; Micah 7:8-10; Haggai 21-23; Zechariah 12:9). With that in mind, I humbly end with the following suggestion:

"If you don't wish to be trampled under God's shoes,
It's a really good idea to be kind to the Jews!"

WORKS CONSULTED

Ausubel, Nathan. *Pictoral History of the Jewish People*. New York: Crown Publishers, 1984.

Birnbaum, Philip. *The Birnbaum Haggadah*. New York: Hebrew Publishing Co., 1976.

Booker, Richard. *How the Cross Became a Sword*. Woodlands, TX: Sounds of the Trumpet, 1994.

Cardozo, Arlene Rossen. *Jewish Family Celebrations: The Sabbath, Festivals, and Ceremonies*. New York: St. Martin's Press, 1982.

Faith Lessons on the Life and Ministry of the Messiah. Vol. 1-4. Dir. Bob Garner and Stephen Stiles. Videocassette. Zondervan Publishing Co., 1998.

Glaser, Mitch and Zhava Glaser. *The Fall Feasts of Israel*. Chicago: Moody Press, 1987.

Hershberger, Ervin N. *Seeing Christ in the Tabernacle*. Meyersdale, PA: Hershberger, 1999.

Hertz, J.H. *Pentateuch & Haftorahs*. 2nd ed. London: Soncino Press, 2001.

Howard, Kevin and Marvin Rosenthal. *The Feasts of the Lord: God's Prophetic Calendar from Calvary to the Kingdom*. Nashville, TN: Thomas Nelson, Inc., 1997.

Kasdan, Barney. *God's Appointed Times: A Practical Guide for Understanding and Celebrating the Biblical Holidays*. Baltimore: Lederer Books, 1993.

Levitt, Zola. *The Miracle of Passover*. Dallas, TX: Levitt, n.d.

—-. *The Seven Feasts of Israel*. Dallas, TX: Levitt, n.d.

Levy, David M. *The Tabernacle: Shadows of the Messiah*. Bellmawr, NJ: The Friends of Israel Gospel Ministry, Inc., 1993.

Miller, Madeleine S. and J. Lane Miller. *Harper's Encyclopedia of Bible Life*. Edison, NJ: Castle Books, 1996.

100 Prophecies Fulfilled by Jesus. n.c.: Rose Publishing, 2002.

Rabinowicz, Rachel Anne, ed. *Passover Haggadah: The Feast of Freedom*. 2nd ed. n.c.: Rabinnical Assembly.

Rosen, Ceil and Moishe Rosen. *Christ in the Passover: Why Is This Night Different?* Chicago: Moody Press, 1978.

Trepp, Leo. *The Complete Book of Jewish Observance: A Practical Manual for the Modern Jew*. New York: Behrman House, Inc./ Summit Books, 1980.

Vamosh, Miriam Feinberg. *Daily Life at the Time of Jesus*. Herzlia, Israel: Palphot, n.d.

CPSIA information can be obtained at www.ICGtesting.com
Printed in the USA
LVOW06s1434280714

396121LV00004B/3/P

9 781609 579296